Our Meal with the Master

Our Meal with the Master

Meditations for the Lord's Supper

James A. Joiner
&
Richard E. White

COVENANT PUBLISHING

www.covenantpublishing.com

P.O. Box 390 Webb City, Missouri 64870
Call toll free at 877.673.1015

Library of Congress Cataloging-in-Publication Data

Joiner, James A. (James Alexander), 1960-
   Our meal with the Master : meditations for the Lord's Supper / James A. Joiner, Richard E. White.
   p. cm.
Includes indexes.
   ISBN 1-892435-24-1 (pbk.)
   1. Lord's Supper—Meditations. I. White, Richard E. (Richard Edgar), 1959- II. Title.
   BV826.5 .J65 2002
   242—dc21
                              2002007514

Table of Contents

Table of Contents

Acknowledgments

The authors would like to thank those who have helped in the formulation of this work and assisted in the editing process. Mr. Robert C. Shannon was kind enough to supply a thoughtful Foreword that clearly presents the purpose for this writing, as well as stating (more eloquently than we) our motivation for conceiving the original idea for this work.

In addition, Mrs. Jean White (Choices) and Mr. Don Beyer (Loss of a Loved One) helped contribute valuable ideas and inspirations. We would also like to thank our wives, Lisa Joiner and Margene White, for their proofreading, critical opinions, and general support for this task. This book would not have been possible without their willingness to endure neglect from their husbands for the completion of this project.

To our children, Hope, Joy, Gina, and Daniel, it is our sincerest prayer that this work will continue to bring you and your children closer to Our Lord long after God has called us home.

Finally, and most importantly, we wish to thank God for instituting the Lord's Supper as a constant reminder of how much He loves us. If the words we have written help bring even a single person closer to the cross of Jesus Christ, then this book will have achieved its purpose.

Foreward

Nothing that we do in worship is more important than Communion. Nothing can do more to make Communion meaningful than a thoughtful and appropriate meditation.

What is needed is a meditation that interprets the Supper for the visitor who may not be familiar with it and at the same time re-interprets it for the person who is very familiar with it. Sometimes it tells us what we already know, but tells it in a different way. Sometimes it tells us what we know, and have been unable to put into words. Sometimes the meditation will speak of things we once knew but have forgotten.

It is obviously difficult to say something fresh about Communion fifty-two times a year. The subject is always the same. While it is difficult, it is not impossible. This book shows us that. The Lord's Supper is a many-faceted diamond and there are more than enough faces for the fifty-two Sundays of the year. With this book as a guide it should be possible for any person to give a Communion meditation and say something that is not predictable and yet is appropriate both in content and in tone.

For all that undertake this task there are some rules. Such meditations should always be brief. There should be no throwaway lines. Every word should be carefully chosen. Every sentence should relate to the topic. And reverence should be the constant keynote.

This book will help enormously to raise the level of this part of our worship. The authors bring two different viewpoints to this meditation. One is an elder. One is a preacher. In a sense we hear a voice from the pulpit and a voice from the pew. While the Communion is in a sense the same for all worshipers, we do view it differently.

–Robert C. Shannon

Preface

Permit us some words of explanation as we begin this book together. We have broken rank with some accepted language authorities by emphasizing certain words with uppercase letters or for the purpose of highlighting the book's theme.

Indexes will help you find subjects, names, and Bible passages. The subjects do not reflect sentiments or like concepts, only specific wording in the text. Hopefully you will be able to find thoughts close enough to what you want to present in your meditation.

We suggest that you keep your comments brief around the Lord's Table, i.e., from three to five minutes. Scripture is the most important aspect of each meditation and should serve as the centerpiece of your comments. Give the gist of the selected writing, not necessarily word for word, to avoid the "cold sound" of a reading. Practice presenting the material and perhaps put it in your own words before you share it with others. You may choose to keep a loose-leaf notebook for additional meditations or appropriate adaptations of the ones listed in this book.

May the Lord bless you as you keep thoughts focused on what Jesus has done for His Body of believers.

A Traitor at the Table

"He who shares my bread has lifted up his heel against me."
John 13:18

Not everyone who sat at the table belonged there. They had followed Him for three years over all the dusty roads and amongst a countless number of faces. They had listened intently to His teachings, at times straining to absorb every word. They'd witnessed glorious miracles and even stood beside Him as others took up stones to kill Him. He was their Master, and they were His closest friends.

Now though, here near the very end, something was wrong. Jesus had just revealed that one of them would soon betray Him. While the others wondered which one of the twelve could possibly do such a thing, Jesus whispered to Judas Iscariot and asked that he do his work quickly. After Judas received the bread from Jesus, he left, a traitor in the night.

What makes this scene all the more ironic is that Judas seems to have occupied the place of honor at the Lord's Table right next to Jesus; even more so was the fact that Jesus had just washed feet that would soon carry a traitor to those plotting Jesus' murder. How could a man like that be invited to the Lord's Table?

There was a time when others also did not belong at the Lord's Table; a time when people like you and me lifted up our heels against Jesus and betrayed His faith and love for us:

> *"…when we were God's enemies, we were reconciled*
> *to him through the death of his Son.…"*
> Romans 5:10

As He once did for Judas, Jesus has washed us also; but He doesn't stop with our feet. He has cleansed all the filth of sin from our hearts and spirits. Once so cleansed, we now have an honored place at the Lord's Table. Today we approach this Table with the confidence of an adopted child, an heir to the salvation given by the Father. But never let it be forgotten that there was a time when we were traitors at this Table; a time not so long ago when we too were children with dirty feet walking in the darkness of sin. As you partake of the Lord's Supper, remember to do so with a grateful heart because the invitation you received to this Table is from a God who decided to destroy His enemies by making them His children.

2

The Price of Victory

They fill the stands and scream. Others prefer to scream at television sets. Regardless of your involvement, athletic events are exciting. But there's a special excitement that only comes if you are a participant in a sporting event. If, as a player, you are fortunate enough to win, you will usually be presented with an award such as a trophy, plaque, medal, or ribbon to commemorate your victory. We usually display these awards in a special place for a period of time where we can view them as a reminder of the victory we achieved. Some businesses, and especially schools, have trophy cases to display their awards and remind us of their many victories. We are a people that seek to be Number One, and rarely are satisfied with anything less. Victory should be achieved no matter what the cost.

The night Jesus instituted the Lord's Supper, He made the statement that has become familiar to all of us:

"...do this in remembrance of me...."

Luke 22:19

So often we remember the crucifixion and the death of our Lord, His broken body and shed blood, and rightly so. But the Communion time for the Christian should also be a time of remembering the victory. While on the cross, Jesus proclaimed:

"It is finished."

John 19:30

This was not a cry of anguish or pain. It was the triumph of victory. Through His death Jesus Christ reconciled us back to God. Even the book of Revelation, no matter what your interpretation, is a book of victory: Jesus Christ is on His throne.

What were you doing there on the sidelines at Calvary? Your real place was out there on the field, at the center of the action. But at the last moment, when the contest appeared hopelessly lost, a Substitution was sent in, and through His action you were awarded the victory. His victory became yours when He lifted your trophy for you. Today as we gather around the bread and the cup, let's remember the victory we have because of Christ: victory over death, sin, and selfishness, and the promise of eternal life.

3
The Greatest Detergent

"It gets out those tough stains." You've heard them, those wonderful claims made by soap companies that tout the superior cleansing abilities of their products. No matter the amount of dirt or how long the stain has set, their great detergent will always wash away all things that stain.

Long before the wisdom of television commercials, the Bible spoke of the world's greatest detergent: *blood*. Medically, the purifying, life-sustaining power of blood is well known. We usually think of blood as being the bearer of oxygen and food to each of our 100 trillion or so cells; but a less glamorous, yet no less vital, function of our blood is garbage collection. In exchange for what it needs, each of your body's cells gives off toxic waste products that must be removed from the cell's immediate environment; otherwise death will occur in a matter of only minutes. In your body there is no life without sanitation, and there is no greater garbage removal system than your bloodstream. Could this be what the Great Physician had in mind when He ordained that

"...without the shedding of blood there is no forgiveness."
Hebrews 9:22

Think of all the garbage and waste that would keep you from being invited to the Lord's Table if it were not for the cleansing blood of Jesus Christ. Not only can The World's Greatest Detergent remove all the toxic waste from your life, but it can do the same for about six billion other people with terrible stains upon their lives. And without the cleansing power of this blood, each of these six billion people will die. Something else about blood too—it really is thicker than water. You can't see through a container of blood like you can a glass of water. Blood makes things disappear. Even our most terrible sins. Isn't it comforting to know that God looks at us through blood-colored glasses; glasses that obliterate our sins, and reveal only the righteousness of Jesus?

As you partake of the cup, do so with the assurance that the Savior's blood has provided not just a life-giving transfusion, but also a cleansing transformation that has removed your sins forever. For:

"...the blood of Jesus, his Son, purifies us from all sin.
1 John 1:7

4
To Take Their Place

One of the greatest blessings a parent receives is that as a mom or dad continues to grow and build a closer relationship with their own children, the insights gained provide better insights into the relationship they have with their own heavenly Father. I was reminded of this several years ago when doctors told me my 3-year-old had to have surgery, and I was faced with the task of telling her why. My problem was: just what words do you use to explain to a young child that she must have an operation and that it's going to hurt a little? Knowing the full impact and seriousness of what lay ahead did not make my task any easier.

I really struggled to find a way to communicate this very serious, important thing so that it could be understood by the mind of a child. And the more I thought about it, the more difficult it became. I remember one particularly frustrating moment when I just shook my head and almost said out loud, "I just wish I could take your place, and put my hand on your shoulder to tell you not to worry, that Daddy was going to take care of everything!"

Not too long afterward, I was reminded that a long time ago another Father was faced with a very similar problem. Oh, He'd given His children guidelines to follow to keep them out of trouble, but as children often do, they chose to ignore them. Then, He sent special messengers and teachers to warn His children what would happen if they didn't listen to Him, but they just couldn't seem to understand the danger that lay ahead; and a number of them just simply refused to listen and ignored the Father's loving discipline. So, finally, being the loving Father that He is, He stooped way down, touched His children's hearts, and said, "Don't worry, Daddy's going to take care of everything for you."

17

Paul tells us that when the time was just right:

*"God sent his Son, born of a woman, born under law, to redeem
those under law, that we might receive the full rights of sons."*
Galatians 4:4

We gather around the Lord's Table to remember that our heavenly Father found a way to take care of our serious problem. When we just weren't able to understand the mess we were really in, He came and took our place. He paid the awful price for sins we committed, because, in the end, it was the only way He could keep us as His children.

So as you partake of the Communion emblems, think about just how much your Father loves you. Think to what extreme He was willing to go in order to protect you and keep you safe from harm. Because when we come around His Table, we are to come as little children and remember the time when our Father stepped down from heaven and made a way to take His children home.

The God Who Hates

*"Take off your sandals, for the place where
you are standing is holy ground."*
Exodus 3:5

We come now to Holy Ground. The reason this ground is holy is because the presence of the Lord is right here with us, and where *He is*, is holy. There's probably no more holy spot on earth than right here around the Communion Table set before us each Lord's Day. Certainly God has a place here; but the amazing thing is that you and I are His honored guests at this holy place.

It's amazing because the absolute holiness of God demands that sin cannot exist in His presence; yet we, of course, are sinners. We readily acknowledge that our Lord is a God of great love and mercy, but how often do we remember that our God is also a God of great hate? The Bible actually contains more Scripture references about God's hate and anger than about His love and tenderness. Psalm 7:11 even tells us:

> *"God is a righteous judge, a God who*
> *expresses his wrath every day."*

What is it then that makes God so angry? Well, the Scriptures tell us that God has a righteous hatred of sin; so much so, that He simply could not bear the thought of those He loves so much coming under the awesome judgment of His holy hatred.

So we come now to remember that singular moment in all of history when God's holy love came face to face with His holy hatred—when His Beloved Son experienced His terrible wrath against the world's sin, and won the ultimate victory over that sin. It was certainly God's love that led Jesus to the cross, but it just might have been God's hatred of sin that helped drive those nails. And that single act is the sacrifice that can cleanse us and make us holy in God's eyes.

The writer of Hebrews 12:14 reveals to us:

> *"…without holiness no one will see the Lord."*

We may also say that without personally accepting the holiness of Christ, neither will you be invited to the Lord's Table. The meal He sets before us is to be shared between a Holy God and His holy people. Don't ever forget that the invitation He extends to you has been engraved in blood, because it's the of blood Jesus Christ that makes us holy as He is holy.

6

Our Covenant Responsibility

"This cup is the new covenant in my blood,
which is poured out for you."

Luke 22:20

Why was the new covenant made with blood? To answer this question we must first understand what a covenant really is. In modern or more common usage, we usually prefer to say "contract" rather than covenant. A contract or covenant requires at least two partners—each with certain responsibilities. For example, most people enter into a covenant with a car dealership. The agreement is that the dealership will provide them with the car of their choice and a warranty of three years or 36,000 miles. The buyer's part of the agreement is then to make a specified monthly payment to the dealership or loan agency. In order for the contract to remain in effect, both parties must abide by the agreement and meet their defined responsibilities.

With a better understanding of a covenant, now let's look at Jesus' statement in Luke. As Christians, we have entered into a contract with Christ. His responsibility: to abolish the burden of the Old Testament law so that we no longer have to live under that law. Instead, the new covenant is a covenant of grace; grace which was personified as Christ shed His own blood on Calvary's cross. Our part of the contract:

"A man ought to examine himself before
he eats of the bread and drinks of the cup."

1 Corinthians 11:28

Christ's covenant with us demands that we examine ourselves to see if we are living as Christ calls us to: a call for holy, forgiving lives lived with integrity.

20

So at this Communion time be reminded that Christ has fulfilled His portion of the covenant. We now live under grace because of His blood. Now comes your part. Examine yourself. Is your lifestyle fulfilling your portion of the covenant written in the Savior's blood?

The Debt that is Paid

Few things in life can match the excitement of driving home a new car. Then that depressingly thick payment book arrives! But one thing that can recapture much of that same excitement is the wonderful feeling that accompanies paying off the loan on that now not-so-new car. What a joy (and relief) it is to know that when that last check is mailed that a long-term debt of several thousand dollars has finally been *paid in full*!

"Jesus said, 'It is finished.' With that,
he bowed his head and gave up his spirit."
John 19:30

These words of Jesus from the cross are usually rendered "It is finished." However, in the original Greek this same word can also be translated another way that just might really convey the reality of what Jesus had done. His last act as a man was to ask for a drink to clear His parched throat, and then He shouted what only God could know, "The debt is paid in full!" Of all the memorable things Jesus might have said here at the very end, why did He choose these specific words? Quite possibly because more than anything else Jesus came to cancel our debt. You see, Jesus forced Himself to endure the agony of the cross until He had paid for every last sin we'll ever commit and for all our failures to follow His example. He took our sins upon Himself, and paid our penalty in full. By doing so,

He canceled our lifelong debts and made us new owners of an inheritance so rich that we can't even begin to comprehend it.

Why is it, He wonders, that we get so excited about paying off a debt to some credit agency, yet often times we're so quick to forget that the greatest debt we'll ever owe—our debt to sin—has been completely paid in full by the sacrificial atonement of the body and blood of Jesus Christ?

The cup and the loaf serve as vivid reminders that the only real debt we owe now is a debt of gratitude & thanksgiving. Not to a creditor, but to a Benefactor that knows we'll never be able to repay. Yet He doesn't care. Never did. What He asks is that we approach His Table with the joy and thanksgiving of a debt-free people; free indeed because He has paid our debt in full.

8

Our Gift to Him

"For to us a child is born, to us a son is given...."
Isaiah 9:6

There's probably nothing as awe-inspiring as being present during the birth of a child. How wonderful it is to witness as a new life filled with hope and promise is born into the world. The birth of Jesus Christ was even more miraculous, yet it was the humility of it all that was so astounding. Instead of a sterile environment surrounded by medical professionals, the King of the Universe was born on the hay of a cow stall surrounded by smelly animals and shepherds from the fields. No movie could have had a more improbable plot: the Hero Who would later save the world born under the most meager of circumstances. Hollywood would have loved it. We remember the scene from the eye of the Scriptures and message of the carols.

A star, a lamb, a mother's hand
Lain upon the Son of Man.
A baby's cry, a lullaby
Sung by loving hearts on high.
For on this night, God's Lamb of Light
Began our journey home.

But behind the stars of nativity, there loomed a dark shadow that had been lurking there from before the beginning.

A smiling face, a child of grace
Born to die, to take our place.
From Eden's fall, to Bethlehem's stall
The cross His purpose, and His call.

Before Jesus Christ felt the warmth of His mother, He felt the nails of His cross. The Lamb of Bethlehem would become the Lion of Judah, but first He must be the Laughingstock of Golgotha. The Communion meal we are about to receive serves to remind us of the agony and shame He endured for us. At Christmas we gladly bring our gifts to the manger, but how often do we remember that it was also our "gifts" that drove Him to decorate our first Christmas tree—His cross? For Him, Bethlehem was the beginning of the end—the end of sin and our separation from God. For us, His birth still provides a new beginning and a new hope.

Salvation's Way in rags and hay,
His crib, but our new birth.

As you gaze at the cup in your hand, remember why red will always be the true color of Christmas.

9
The Bread that Reveals

They'd taken this seven-mile journey many times before, but this time things were different. As these disciples slowly made their way down the winding, well-traveled road, their minds kept drifting back to Jerusalem. They'd witnessed it all, yet the reality of His death just wouldn't sink in. Their minds fought against accepting it. They had believed in Him. Jesus of Nazareth, "a prophet powerful in word and deed," now lived only in their memories; and memories, no matter how vivid, could never bring Him back. Their hopes were as empty as His tomb. At least John and Peter had verified that part of the women's story. But the body... There was nothing left now but to go home, get on with their lives, and wait for the real Messiah.

A mile or so west of Jerusalem He joined them. They were amazed at His ignorance of what just happened at Passover, but were set afire as He expounded the wisdom of the ages. At journey's end they insisted that this compelling Stranger stay and share their evening meal, and even asked Him to be the host at the Table. As the Stranger broke the bread and gave it to them, eyes that had refused to see were suddenly opened to reveal the risen Lord they had abandoned along the road to Emmaus.

> "When he was at the table with them, he took bread,
> gave thanks, broke it and began to give it to them.
> Then their eyes were opened and they recognized him...."
> Luke 24:30-31

If Jesus walked the earth today, how would you recognize Him? What would it take to open your eyes? One important reason Jesus came to earth was to reveal what God is like; and amidst all the power, passion, and purpose maybe Jesus is most visible in the simplest of acts—like the breaking of bread at the dinner table.

"This is my body given for you.…"

Luke 22:19

Like those disciples, we too come to receive bread from Jesus. But there's a difference. This bread not only reveals the true identity of the One who breaks it, but also reveals the heart of a God who refused to be a stranger. We walk with Him today because He once walked alone for us. As your eyes are closed in prayer, remember that God has broken much more than bread at this Table. Through the sacrificial death of Jesus Christ your bondage to sin has been forever broken, and He has revealed the incomprehensible love that led to a cross. Once your spiritual eyes are opened and you fully appreciate what He has done for you, you'll never have to walk alone again.

10
Choices

When God made man He gave us a brain to be used to make the best choices, but Adam and Eve chose to have it their way and do what was forbidden by God. Their second choice was to blame others for their own disobedience. Interesting that man's first choice is the same one we've been making ever since. Although times certainly change, humanity rarely does. As we grow up we are to learn to make good choices. We choose how much schooling, whom to fall in love with, whom to marry, and how many children we want. We choose our lifestyle and our friends. Like Adam and Eve, we even choose whether or not we will obey God. Perhaps this morning you chose between rising late to spend

Sunday morning with a pot of coffee and a newspaper, or spending it with fellow Christians in Bible study and worship. Unlike our ancestors, we pray we will always make the right choices.

Jesus Christ was the only person born with "no choice." Yet we know that He chose to carry out His Father's will, and that divine will was clear from before the beginning. Jesus knew He was

> *"the Lamb that was slain from the creation of the world."*
> Revelation 13:8

Before He hung the earth amidst the heavenlies, Jesus Christ knew He would be hung on a cross. Yet He chose to enter this world and complete the work ordained by His Father. The choice of Bethlehem was also the certainty of Calvary. Even as a young man He had no choice but "to be about His Father's business." This time though, no serpent could prevent the choosing of a life lived in perfect obedience to the will of God. Although His mortal nature struggled in the blood of Gethsemene and was horrified at the prospect of the "cup" set before Him, He made God's choice and went to the cross willingly so that you and I could have the choice of eternal life.

> *"See I set before you today life and prosperity, death and*
> *destruction.... Now choose life, so that you and your children*
> *may live and that you may love the LORD your God, listen*
> *to his voice, and hold fast to him. For the LORD is your life...."*
> Deuteronomy 30:15, 19-20

The emblems set before us at this Communion Table represent Jesus' life, suffering, and dying, and were instituted by Him just before He went to the cross. Because of His choice, we now have the choice to love. Thank Him for that costly forgiveness, and strive to live a life patterned after His own. If you choose to partake, then contemplate the price He paid just so you could have the right to choose.

The Cups of Jesus

"Father, if you are willing, take this cup from me…"
Luke 22:42

As the last night of His earthly life was coming to an end, Jesus asked that His cup be taken. In the Garden His Father was asked to remove Jesus' cup of suffering, and while still in the upper room Jesus had asked His disciples to receive the cup representing the new covenant between God and man. Though the cups were offered for different purposes, both represented the blood of Jesus. In one, blood that would soon be shed in death. In the other, blood that would seal the salvation of life eternal. Two cups, two requests, but only one blood.

At the traditional Passover meal shared by Jesus and His disciples, four cups of wine were offered to commemorate God's fourfold promise to Israel in Exodus 6:6-7: promise of *relief, release, redemption,* and *relationship.* That is, relief from the burdens imposed by the Egyptians, release from the bondage of slavery, and redemption through His great acts and power. Finally, God would seek a relationship with these people He called His own. At the Last Supper the cup offered by Jesus is thought to have been the third ceremonial cup, or "Cup of Blessing." Just as His disciples' thoughts were now focused on the redeeming power of God, Jesus was teaching them that their redemption and greatest blessing would come through His own blood. His terrible cup would soon be filled with the wrath of a God determined to destroy the power of all sin and rebellion, yet through this same cup He would make a loving God personal. This time the road to redemption would not be the Red Sea, but a new way stained red with blood. Instead of the waters, a veil of separation would be divided. A cross would be this Good

27

Shepherd's staff of miracles.

"I will take you as my own people, and I will be your God."
Exodus 6:7

Notice Who takes the active role in building this relationship. God has been freeing slaves for quite a long time. It is He that now offers each of us a cup of redemption, and the cup before us today reminds us that our days of slavery to sin are at an end. But that's just the beginning. Jesus' gracious blood also relieves sin's penalty and makes it possible for you to have your own personal relationship with God. So now, join those early followers in taking the cup of blessing offered by Jesus. But as you partake, remember the other cup. Jesus' Garden cup was not really His to give. It was your sinful cup He drank from on the cross; a cup filled with God's judgment, sin's defeat, our redemption, and His blood.

"Shall I not drink the cup the Father has given me?"
John 18:11

Family Ties

For many of us the fondest memories we treasure are those times spent with our families. We even set aside special times during our busy year for family reunions and other get-togethers where we exchange stories and renew our ties with those closest to us. These bonds that reach across the years and across long distances are usually the strongest personal relationships we have, resulting in a very special love we share with those who are related to us. Oh, we may disagree from time to time, but there's no denying the power of that unique tie that holds a family together. Like our natural families, our Christian family also has a special "Glue" that holds it together.

> *"I kneel before the Father, from whom his whole*
> *family in heaven and on earth derives its name."*
> Ephesians 3:14-15

The Greek word for "family" comes from the word "father." It is the father that gives a family its name, and is to provide for the needs of his family. Our heavenly Father has done all this and so much more. You see, at one time we were "spiritual orphans," separated from the family of God. Even more than that, Paul tells us in Romans 5:10 that all those outside of God's family are actually enemies of God. Can you imagine the terrible implications of being an enemy of Almighty God? But instead of keeping us as hopeless children of wrath, God provided a way to adopt us into His family.

> *"You are all sons of God through faith in Christ Jesus,*
> *or all of you who were baptized into Christ have clothed*
> *yourselves with Christ.… for you are all one in*
> *Christ Jesus.… and heirs according to the promise."*
> Galatians 3:27-29

Think of what it took to transform you from an enemy into an heir, from being God's foe to becoming God's family. Family ties are strong because families are bound together by the sharing of blood. We speak of "blood relations" or "blood line," the idea being that there's something very powerful in the blood that binds families together. As we gather around the Lord's Table, think of it not only as a time of Communion, but also a time of *reunion*; a time when the entire family of God comes together to be reminded of the wonderful tie that binds us all together in our Father's family—the blood of Jesus Christ.

Signposts

As you drive, oftentimes you see road signs posted along the way that serve as *indicators*—signs like "Dangerous Curve Ahead" or "Speed Detected by Radar" or even "Children Playing" serve to remind us to drive safely and to obey the traffic laws. Without such roadside reminders it would be easy for us to lose our way, have an accident, or even lose our lives or take the lives of others; not to mention the indignity and cost of receiving a traffic ticket.

The Lord's Supper is also an indicator or sign that helps us navigate the road of life. All the important reminders are there. At the Lord's Table we see God's justice demanding that all transgressions be paid for, but we also come face to face with the One who served our sentence for us. As we gather together, we of course recall the words of Jesus *". . . do this in remembrance of me"*; words that bring to mind His love and sacrifice. But there are also other areas of living that Christ wants us to remember at this Communion time.

Jesus told a parable about mercy and forgiveness in Matthew 18:21-35. In verse 33 Jesus said:

> *"Shouldn't you have had mercy on your*
> *fellow servant just as I had on you?"*

When was the last time you showed mercy to someone? The man in Jesus' parable was shown unlimited mercy as his tremendous debt was canceled, yet this forgiven man refused to extend any forgiveness to his debtor. The Master reminds us that an unmerciful heart costs us more than we'll ever know. Since we have received His unlimited mercy, how can we not extend that same mercy to others? This Communion time reminds us of our abundant blessing of grace, but also emphasizes our divine obligation to forgive our debtors "seventy times seven" if necessary.

The other area is love for our brothers and sisters in Christ. We are told in 1 John 4:11 that since we have been loved by the Father,

"we also ought to love one another."

This is not love born of passion, nor just a brotherly love; it is *agape* love that must seek the absolute best for others at any cost. This was the magnitude of the love extended to us on the cross, and the kind of love the Master expects us to show for our fellow man.

The road Jesus walked was clearly marked by signs indicating the danger just ahead; but He ignored these signs and suffered at the hands of those who refused to show mercy or love. Let the Lord's Supper be a sign for you—a sign reminding you to live a life filled with mercy and love. When you're reminded of what Jesus did for you, how can you do otherwise?

14
Remembering to Forget

In our modern, mobile society very few of us live out our lives in a single community. As we continue to develop or change careers and later retire, we often pull up our roots to set them down in another town or state. In the face of all this change, however, is a constant that we find wherever we go—the Church of Jesus Christ. For most of us, finding a new church home is a top priority as we settle into a new city; and nothing reminds the Christian of "being home more than those familiar words inscribed on nearly every Communion Table:

"...do this in remembrance of me...."

1 Corinthians 11:24

The key word in this important command of Jesus is "remember." The Lord's Table is set before us as a memorial; and like all memorials we are to pause and reflect upon the significance of what it means. But remembering means more than simply "bringing to mind"; it carries with it the idea of carefully considering and taking into account the importance of events remembered. The emblems on the Communion Table are tangible reminders of past payment for our future inheritance.

Yet remembering is not really the central theme of Communion. This Table is primarily a memorial to forgetting. Listen to what God says about His new covenant:

> *"For I will forgive their wickedness and*
> *will remember their sins no more."*
> Jeremiah 31:34b

As Christians we are taught to be a forgiving people, and most of us have little problem with accepting a sincere apology. On the other hand, think about how difficult it is for you to forget—to have a wrong completely removed from your memory. We seldom hold onto grudges, yet grudgingly resist forgetting things entirely. God, thankfully, is different. Certainly one of the most amazingly wonderful things about our Heavenly Father is that He not only forgives, but also forgets our sins completely. All those immersed into Jesus Christ are covered by His blood, the real agent of God's forgetfulness. Sins that should have stained us forever are now forever hidden by our new clothes:

> *"For he has clothed me with garments of salvation*
> *and arrayed me in a robe of righteousness...."*
> Isaiah 61:10

How could God be so blind? Actually, God overlooks our sins because He alone sees the true cleansing power in the blood of His Son; and the real power in this blood becomes the power to forget. As you come to this most special memorial follow the directions written in the

Table and remember; but remember that it's because of the blood of Jesus Christ that God can forget.

15
The Bondage of Freedom

On June 4, 1865, just weeks after the American Civil War had ended, a newly freed Black American walked into a church service and raised quite a few eyebrows. During the observance of the Lord's Supper, much to the shock of many members in attendance that morning, this former slave walked down the aisle and knelt at the Communion Table. After a few moments of uneasy silence, an older white gentleman with a gray beard arose and came to the front of the church in his customary dignified manner, and knelt down to partake of Communion near the one who had so boldly stepped forward. Although he offered not a word, his message was clear; and those in attendance that morning always remembered the lesson they were taught when a former slave and former Confederate General Robert E. Lee knelt at the Lord's Table together as simple servants of the same Master.

Many years before the apostle Paul wrote of the Christian's deliverance from slavery and of our unity in Jesus Christ:

> *"You are all sons of God through faith in Christ Jesus....*
> *There is neither Jew nor Greek, slave nor free,*
> *male nor female, for you are all one in Christ Jesus."*
> Galatians 3:26-28

Before Jesus Christ came to die for us, we were all captives under the slavery of sin. Yet Jesus did not really come to abolish our servitude; instead, He only demands that we change Masters.

*"But thanks be to God that, though you used to be
slaves to sin.... you have been set free from sin and
have become slaves to righteousness.... and have
become slaves to God... and the result is eternal life."*

Romans 6:18,22

A slave has no real will of his own, and is little more than the tool of his master. With sin as our master we had no choice but death. But then He Who offers true freedom became our slave and shouldered our terrible burden for us. We and our brothers and sisters in Christ come to kneel before a Communion Table that offers us freedom freely granted by our new Master; but let us not forget that purchasing a slave always cost something. Our freedom cost our Master dearly. And now that we are freed from the penalty of our sin, we are free to become slaves of God. What a wonderful paradox it is that the freedom of God can only be experienced by those who become slaves to righteousness. No matter your background or occupation, we all kneel before Him today because He was once lifted up for us.

16
We Were There

We were there watching as He destroyed the darkness. The authority of His voice echoed across that vast emptiness and the universe became. As we watched the stars come to life and the planets begin marking out their orbits, we simply could not be silent:

*"...while the morning stars sang together
and all the angels shouted for joy?"*

Job 38:7

We erupted in joyful praise to the Creator for His work of forming such grandeur out of absolute nothingness. How privileged we were to have been there to witness this greatest of miracles.

We were also there watching on that magical night when He decided to introduce Himself to His creation. We struggled to try and comprehend this miracle of miracles—the Eternal One taking on the flesh and limitations of the creature. But not one of us fully realized what was unfolding before us. Surely the earth could not be silent this night; but if the earth would not sing His praise then we would. Once again we filled the skies with our doxology.

> *"Suddenly a great company of the heavenly host*
> *appeared with the angel, praising God and saying,*
> *'Glory to God in the highest....'"*
>   Luke 2:13-14

It didn't matter that only the shepherds heard us, for there had to be praise to welcome the Creator on this night. Surely this was His greatest miracle of all: the night that time was touched by eternity. And above it all, again, was a star He created.

But one day we waited near a lonely hill longing for a call that never came. This time His beautiful stars had vanished as darkness transformed our anthems of joy into silent tears of sorrow. Angels aren't supposed to cry, but as we watched the Father turn away from His Son, the Creator bleeding for the creature's sin, it was more than any of us could bear. As He hung there so alone, we began to realize that this was indeed His greatest miracle—a miracle of love.

Instead of His cross, you now come around His Table. Instead of stars, there is a loaf and a cup to remind you that the Creator is still performing miracles today. But there are no more universes to fashion. Now His miracle is *creating nothing out of something,* that is, completely removing the sin that once darkened your life. We once sang amongst the stars, but now you can be a star that points the way to Him. As you partake in the quietness of this moment, listen closely and you just might hear those same angelic songs coming from within your own heart.

17

From Rags to Righteousness

There are two things we all seem to have; one is a junk drawer to store our "stuff," the other a comfortable old T-shirt that is now just a rag. For some of us, getting rid of that favorite T-shirt, no matter how bad it looks, is not an easy thing. Oftentimes we refuse to use that particular rag because it used to be my "best T-shirt." But I have noticed that for many of us once we designate that shirt as a rag (even if we never use it) we just can't seem to make ourselves wear it because now "it is a rag." No matter how many times we wash, bleach, sterilize, or purify, it is a garment that will never be worn again.

God's Word is clear that everyone is clothed in something. In Isaiah 64:6 we are told:

> *"All of us have become like one who is unclean,*
> *and all our righteous acts are like filthy rags...."*

As we approach the Communion time, let's be reminded that it was not *our* actions that brought salvation, but the one righteous act of Christ on the cross that provides us with eternal life. At one time we were clothed in rags of our own making, but no matter how hard we tried these garments could never be "good enough." Just as a person wearing only filthy rags would never be accepted into a fine restaurant or place of business, we could never hope to gain entrance into God's Kingdom by way of our own righteousness. Instead, there had to be a divine makeover that put our "righteousness" in its proper place "nailed to a filthy cross." The work of Jesus now clothes us in His righteousness, which we are to wear proudly as a beautiful breastplate (Ephesians 6:14). Quite a transformation has occurred—from our filthy rags of death to a polished, protective garment that gives us the certainty of life eternal.

Yet unlike that ragged old T-shirt we refuse to go back and put on, many of us occasionally sort through life's junk drawer and slip back into those filthy rags Jesus once wore for us. Communion time challenges us not to re-cover ourselves with any self-made righteousness, not to live by the flesh any more, but to live under the blood of Jesus that purifies us from all our sins and confers upon us the very righteousness of God's Holy Son.

Let this Lord's Supper remind us about all Christ went through to dispose of our disgusting rags and give us new garments that represent forgiveness of our sins and provide us with eternal life.

18

Living on Main Street

In most towns there is a main street; and when Main Street was originally named it was exactly that—the primary street that was the center of a town's commerce. But today in many cities Main Street is anything but the "main street." The outward growth of cities has pushed many businesses and governmental offices out of the downtown area, so that Main Street is no longer a priority in the lives of many citizens. Still, the concept of a main street has not disappeared completely; there are towns where Main Street remains the center of the city's life.

For most of us when we first accepted Christ as our Savior it was easy to fix Him at the center of our lives, to make Him our "Main Street." But far too often we let the busy-ness and cares of the world push Jesus out to the more remote areas of our lives. Oh, we know He's still there because we're so quick to confess Him as our personal Savior that has opened heaven's door for us; but confessing Him as the Lord of our lives, the center of our everyday walk—well, that's often quite a different matter. How easy it is for you and me to relegate Jesus to the "suburbs" of our lives while we seek worldly comfort and happiness. Like our modern society, we've forgotten our Main Street which remains the true source of all the real joy and necessities of life.

In the Scriptures we see that God's people must choose to live on Main Street by turning aside from any of life's side streets, and this turning often demands a radical departure from old ways, experiences, and habits. For the one who drops everything to follow Jesus

> *"is a new creation; the old has gone, the new has come!"*
> 2 Corinthians 5:17

Before he set out on Main Street, Elisha killed his oxen and burned his plow (1 Kings 19:21). Four successful businessmen, Peter, Andrew, James, and John, immediately dropped their assets to follow the call of Christ (Matthew 1:18-22). For these men there was no turning back to old ways. The divine call to walk on Main Street is to be final, and must involve hating any alternative routes. It is the way of the cross, both for Jesus and all who dare to follow in His footsteps (Luke 14:26-27).

Let your eyes follow the main aisle of the sanctuary to where it all begins—at the Communion Table. Your Host at this meal invites you to resolve that this new way will be your "Main Street" for the remainder of your days. The Lord's Supper, without a doubt, forces you to determine what part of your life you'll allow Christ to hold in His hands. Is He your "Main Street," or do you only come to Him when it's time to have spiritual bills paid? Now as you gather around this Table the age old challenge is again renewed: "Is Christ the main priority of your life?" He wants to be—that's why He died, paving your life's Main Street with His own blood.

19

The Joy of Sadness

At times things in life just don't seem to make a lot of sense—at least at first glance. For instance, there are a number of things that bring both joy and sadness into our lives. Some examples would be the satisfactions and time demands of our chosen profession, that favorite team that takes us on emotional roller coaster rides, children that enliven and sometimes exasperate our lives, and even animals that we adopt into our families as pets. Cats are a great example. They can be a joy as they patrol our homes during the night to keep unwanted animals out of the house, but they can also drive you crazy wanting in and out of the house at 3:00 in the morning. Wonder if God mixes things up a little just to keep life interesting for us?

There are also examples of things and people expressing surprisingly positive reactions to "negative" circumstances in Scripture. For example, Jesus' apostles often rejoiced in their own suffering of physical pain and public disgrace (e.g., Acts 5:41). On a more personal level, James tells us to consider it all joy when we face various trials (James 1:1). But probably the most perfect paradox was Jesus Christ Himself being both God and man at the same time. Certainly His was a life of joy and sadness; and there is a unique verse that describes a single event in His life that was filled with both these strong emotions:

> *"…Jesus, the author and perfecter of our faith,*
> *who for the joy set before him endured the cross.…"*
> Hebrews 12:2

We don't normally consider joy as something to be "endured," but in the context of the cross, it makes perfect sense. This passage goes on to tell us that Christ endured the shame of the cross, but received joy as He sat down at the right hand of the throne of God. We might also add that His great joy of finally restoring our relationship with our Father gave Him the endurance to withstand the agony of the cross.

On the Table before us are two emblems, and we might consider that one represents joy and the other, sorrow. The bread reminds us that we are now all of the same Body; now all family bound together in the joy of the One who has forever linked us to the Father. In contrast, the juice from crushed grapes never lets us forget the time our Lord gave His very blood so that we could belong to His Body. From now on every joy we experience in our Christian lives is a joy born out of His sorrow and suffering. The charge before for us this and every morning is to now spread His joyful love throughout an otherwise sad, sinful world. With joy He gave His life; with all our lives, let's work to bring Him joy.

20

Restoration

"It hurts!" That's the lasting memory many of us have of a broken arm or other injury to one of our limbs. In addition to the pain, an injured or dislocated arm is totally useless because either you cannot move it, or it hurts so much that you don't dare move it. In order to mend the arm it must be immobilized and restored to it's proper state, i.e., the bones set so they will knit together properly or the normal orientation in the shoulder joint reestablished. Of course, the first step in the healing process is getting to a trained specialist who knows exactly how to restore the limb and has the necessary equipment to do so. Setting broken bones or restoring dislocated joints is just not something you can do to yourself.

In contrast to the Emergency Room physician, the Great Physician is in the business of restoring more than just broken arms and legs. Many years ago David wrote of God's great powers of restoration.

The LORD is my shepherd, I shall not be in want.
He makes me lie down in green pastures,
he leads me beside quiet waters, he restores my soul."
Psalm 23:1-3

The New Testament Greek word for "restoring" or "reconciling" God's people was the same word used by physicians to describe the setting of broken bones or mending of a dislocated body part. The analogy is an ideal one to help us understand the full impact of the saving work of Jesus Christ. Before His healing work on the cross, our fellowship with God was completely broken. What's more, just as a broken arm cannot follow any instructions from the head, we were completely useless to God and did not obey His commandments. But God looked down upon our hopeless state and sent His Son to restore us to the proper fellowship for which we were first created. Jesus set our broken lives and then used His own cross as a splint on which to heal the pain of our fractured and strained relationship with His and our Father. You can probably remember the gratitude you expressed to your physicians and nurses after they helped rid your body of an illness, but do you remember the last time you sincerely thanked Jesus Christ for the restoration your soul?

The Communion Table set before us is a table of healing and restoration. Here you will find reminders of the instruments Jesus used to reconcile us to God: His body and blood. His was the greatest miracle of heart surgery ever performed. But one thing is still lacking. As powerful as He is, Jesus can only heal if the patient is willing. Remember, Jesus Christ is still in the business of restoring precious souls and fitting them for God's service. When you come to realize the tremendous cost of His commitment to heal your soul, how can you commit anything less than your very best to Him?

It's Just Not Fair

Few things in life irritate a parent as much as hearing those terrible words, "She got more than I did. It's not fair!" As much as we struggle to instill appreciation and gratitude into our children, we find that human nature is such a stubborn thing. We are born seeking what we want, and wanting it precisely when we want it. But maybe the most frustrating thing is that we never really grow out of this attitude. Even as we "mature," how much effort do we still expend "keeping up with the Joneses" or feeling slighted when that special promotion goes to a coworker instead of to me? We all want what we consider to be our fair share, and how quickly our righteous indignation rises when we believe life has slighted us unfairly.

How ironic it is that we demand to be treated fairly, yet we gladly accept the greatest unfairness of all. Jesus Christ died so that we would not receive what we deserved. It wasn't fair, but it was God's will.

> *"He made Him who knew no sin to be sin on our behalf,*
> *so that we might become the righteousness of God in Him."*
> 2 Corinthians 5:21 (NASB)

Here is the most astounding inequity of all: Jesus becoming our sin, while we become His righteousness. In this covenant neither party was treated fairly, but we certainly don't complain about it, do we? In theological terms we call this grace and joyfully sing of it as being "Amazing," "Wonderful," and "Marvelous"; but in reality the best adjective to describe grace is "Unfair." We love to speak of the infinite attributes of our God, but so often we forget to praise Him for His amazing unfairness. Of course, His righteousness demands that all sin be paid for; it's just that He chose to put aside fairness and suffer our punishment. Sometimes we are so quick to question God when we suffer illness, lose a job, or lose a loved one, but rarely pause to question Him about the unfairness of our abundant blessings. Something is very wrong here; and He's the One to blame.

As we come around His Table maybe it's time to learn from our children and recognize that "It's just not fair!" As you receive the cup and the loaf, contemplate the wondrous injustice committed by God at Calvary, and the awesome love that allowed His only Son to receive the death penalty we so richly deserved. Jesus never asked for an appeal on the grounds of fairness, but whoever said God was fair?

22
You Can Take It with You

She lived a long life, enjoying children, grandchildren, and even great-grandchildren, and then like most of us was finally called home. Services were held in a peaceful cemetery on a hillside overlooking a beautiful valley. After the brief service at the base of the mountain, they climbed the hillside and paused for a moment to gaze at the mountains and watch the final preparations below. The friends and family had all gone now, and the workers were making the final preparations. And there, just for a moment, the questions came: "Is that all there is to life?" "No matter what you do in life, is this eventually how it will end?" "Is there really any purpose to life at all?"

It was at that moment that God spoke. Just a few feet from where she was buried, stood a large white marble statue of Jesus with His arms outstretched to welcome His children home. In silence the statue spoke to everyone, letting them know that there really is an eternal purpose to our temporary lives. There is something we take with us when we depart this life; anything done for God while on earth follows us into heaven.

There is great peace in knowing that all those in Christ are safe in His arms, where one day we'll gather around a Lord's Table not built by human hands.

> *"And I confer on you a kingdom, just as my Father*
> *conferred one on me, so that you may eat and*
> *drink at my table in my kingdom...."*
> Luke 22:29-30

But we come around a different Lord's Table; one not only built *by* human hands, but, more importantly, one built *because* of human hands; because of our sin. This Table serves to remind us that the reason Jesus will one day welcome us into heaven with open arms is because those same arms were once stretched out and nailed to a cross for you and for me. The cup and the loaf aren't here to remind us of a beautiful marble statue in a peaceful valley, but of a Savior who died on a lonely hill so we never will. And it's because of the gracious love that made this Table that one day we'll all be gathered around that heavenly Table where death and tears are forever washed away.

23
The Miracle of Easter

We assemble together to worship a God of miracles; and His miracles are all around us. From the stars up in the sky to the person sitting there in church beside you, the world is full of God's miracles. Miracles are signs that point us to God, but so often we take them for granted. It's surprising that when you read the Gospels you find that the only people expecting an empty tomb that first Easter morning were the ones that had plotted Jesus' murder. Jesus' followers, sadly, expected no miracle.

Thomas would believe only what he saw, while Peter and Mary actually looked into the tomb but still refused to believe what they saw. As we gather beside an empty tomb, what kind of miracle do you see?

Many would consider the resurrection of Jesus Christ to be the greatest miracle of all. Others might say that God's greatest miracle was the time when He reached down from His throne and out into empty space to create something where there once was nothing. But as we gather around the Lord's Table, we're reminded that just maybe God's greatest miracle of all was when He reached into the sin and darkness of your own heart and replaced it with the joy and light of His own Spirit. At this Table, we're reminded not of a miraculous universe, or even an empty tomb; what we see before us now is the miracle of an old rugged cross.

Paul tells us in 1 Corinthians 1:22-24:

> *"Jews demand miraculous signs and Greeks look for wisdom, but we preach Christ crucified: a stumbling block to Jews and foolishness to Gentiles, but to those whom God has called, both Jews and Greeks, Christ the power of God and the wisdom of God."*

Like that empty tomb the power and curse of death is gone from our lives, and Jesus has personally rolled away any barrier between His heavenly Father and us. As you receive the bread and the cup, remember that the miracle of the cross is a miracle of love; a love that makes the miracle and joy of Easter Sunday live in our hearts every day of the year.

24

Dirty Hands

He'd spent most of the day Saturday outside staining some woodwork; but after the day's work was done and things were cleaned, he noticed his hands were still spotted with the dark stain that would hopefully be gone in a few days. He thought no more about his stains until he arrived at church the following morning and a friend commented about the marks on his "dirty" hands. A few jokes were made, but nothing more was said about his hands during Bible class. His dirty hands continued to go unnoticed through the song service. But as the Communion tray was passed and he reached out to take the bread and the cup, he just couldn't help noticing those dark, black stains on his hands. It was at that moment that he realized just how dirty his hands really were. You see, although his hands weren't very good at carpentry or painting, there once was a time when those same hands were more than enough to nail Jesus Christ to a tree. Dirty hands that helped shed innocent blood.

After Cain murdered his innocent brother, God told him:

> *"Now you are under a curse and driven from*
> *the ground, which opened its mouth to receive*
> *your brother's blood from your hand."*
> Genesis 4:11

Later, David passed judgment on those who spilt innocent blood:

> *"...when wicked men have killed an innocent*
> *man... should I not now demand his blood*
> *from your hand and rid the earth of you!"*
> 2 Samuel 4:11

David had these guilty men killed, and actually cut off their hands. That's how serious their stains were! But our hands aren't really much cleaner than theirs, are they? We too have helped shed innocent blood. But the amazing thing is that these same hands that once put Jesus on His cross, are now invited to fellowship at His Table. Instead of being cursed and cut off, our hands have been cleansed!

So as you slowly reach your hand toward Jesus' bread and cup, pause just a moment to think about the "spiritual stains" on your own hands; and rejoice because the blood of Jesus has forever washed away all those terrible stains.

In God We Trust

Behold the penny. Used to be, if you saw one of these on the ground, you'd pick it up. For a child, that meant you were now rich. For an adult, if nothing else, it was a good luck charm. Nowadays though, few people will take the time to bend down and pick up a penny because in today's society a single penny is considered to be fairly worthless. But if you look at it closely, you'll find something that makes this little coin invaluable. Right above Lincoln's head these words are inscribed, "In God We Trust." It may very well be because of these four little words that the United States of America is blessed as the world's greatest nation.

Herein lies our history. When a young George Washington was leaving home to begin a life of public service, his mother's parting words were, *"Remember, My son, that God is our only sure trust."* As Abraham Lincoln was leaving Illinois for Washington, he spoke these words, *"Without the assistance of God, I cannot succeed. With that assistance I cannot fail. Trusting in Him let us confidently hope that all will be well."* It was Lincoln's Treasury secretary, Salmon Chase, who wrote: *"No nation can be strong except in the strength of God. The trust of our people in God should be declared on our national coins."* That's why "In God We Trust" is printed here. Over 100 years later President Ronald Reagan reaffirmed our Christian heritage, *"The time has come to turn to God and reassert our trust in Him."* So you see, this little is coin is pretty valuable after all.

We come now to that most special time in our worship service when we declare, "In God We Trust." Unlike a penny, it is not written above our heads; instead, it's inscribed on our hearts. The apostle Paul spoke of this special trust that we have in God:

> *"Indeed, in our hearts we felt the sentence of death. But this happened that we might not rely on ourselves but on God, who raises the dead. He has delivered us from such a deadly peril, and he will deliver us. On him we have set our hope that he will continue to deliver us...."*
>
> 2 Corinthians 1:9-10

The Table we gather around now reminds us that we have been delivered; not from a foreign nation, but from the oppression of sin. Each of us has earned sin's wages, yet we receive the Grace of God through the Gift of His Son who died so we might live. The cup and the loaf we take now are here to remind us of both the cost and the joy of the salvation we receive when "In God We Trust."

26
The Broken Pieces

Humpty-Dumpty sat on a wall; Humpty-Dumpty had a great fall. It was over for Humpty-Dumpty. Only broken pieces were left, and no earthly power—neither kings nor things—were able to give any meaning to those shattered remains. The precarious lives of many people are not unlike that of Humpty-Dumpty. Any life set upon a wall built of pride, possessions, or power must eventually fall and be broken. This kind of wall climbing leads only to ruin.

Unlike the Humpty-Dumpties of the world, however, brokenness is the point at which a Christian's life truly begins. To appreciate the holiness and perfection of God is to come face to face with the depravity and need of one's own soul. Listen to the words of those great heroes of the Faith, Isaiah and Paul:

> *"'Woe to me!' I cried. 'I am ruined! For I am a man of unclean lips, and I live among a people of unclean lips, and my eyes have seen the King, the Lord Almighty.'"* Isaiah 6:5

> *"What a wretched man I am! Who will rescue me from this body of death?"* Romans 7:24

Before God can make us, He first has to break us. Those who would live for God must first die to the world. But does God ask too much of us? How can He possibly take the broken pieces of our lives and make them whole again? There is an answer. God can put us back together because He was once broken for us.

> *"This is my body, which is for you...."* 1 Corinthians 11:24

Communion time is a vivid reminder for us that as Jesus Christ was broken, we were made whole. This is no nursery rhyme. The death of this King has done what no earthly king could ever do. The perfect standard of God's law is a wall that shatters the "goodness" of all people; no one can climb a wall of works into heaven. At the foot of this wall, all is broken. Instead of scaling a wall, we must kneel at a cross. As you now break the bread, remember to lay down the pieces of your old, broken life. Life eternal is yours because God nailed those broken pieces to a cross where a Savior was broken so we could be made whole.

27
The Cost of Sacrifice

As we look back over the pages of the Old Testament, we find very specific rules about making an offering or a sacrifice to the Lord. The first recorded offerings were those of Cain and Abel back in Genesis Chapter 4. As you remember the story, the Lord was pleased with Abel's sacrifice, but Cain's offering was rejected. Although we're not told specifically why this was so, it might have been because Cain's bloodless sacrifice consisted of just leftover portions of his crop. Abel, instead, offered the very best of his firstborn flock. One offering, a priority that cost the giver something; the other, probably just an afterthought that cost the giver little.

As Christians, we too are to give back a portion of our material blessings to God. But are our monetary offerings really pleasing to God? If we have our health and our job, we can always make more money; it's our time that's really more precious. Once passed, it's gone forever. Because our time and commitment are more costly, maybe they are actually more acceptable sacrifices to God.

God speaks about the importance of the cost of a sacrifice. Listen to His words:

> *"Cursed is the cheat who has an acceptable male in*
> *his flock and vows to give it, but then sacrifices a*
> *blemished animal to the Lord. For I am a great King...."*
> Malachi 1:14

Why is God so picky? Is He being unreasonable when He seems so adamant about accepting only our very best? The answer can probably be found right here at the Table set before us. One of the reasons we come here every Lord's Day is to remember that day long ago when God gave His very best for you and me. He didn't just offer us a bowl of fruit or write us out a check; God gave the One most dear to Him, His only Son, to be our sacrifice: a perfect, spotless, and blameless sacrifice that cost Jesus His life.

So as we now receive the cup and the loaf, let's remember just how precious this moment is. For it is here that we come face to face with the One Who gave His all to prepare this meal for us. And it's through His costly sacrifice of love that you and I can know just how precious we are to God. In death, He gave us the very best He had to offer so that you and I could become a living sacrifice for Him.

28

Beauty and Purpose

Wind chimes are amazing things. They are designed with a very specific purpose, but also retain a unique beauty. Wind chimes come in many shapes and sizes, and are made of quite a diversity of materials. Some are made of seashells, while others are made of brass; still others are made of glass, and the list could go on and on. In addition to the variety of materials, wind chimes also come in different colors and designs. All of these things make them beautiful, depending on your likes and dislikes. But no matter the shape, size, or material, the wind chime has a specific purpose: to create a beautiful music from the invisible power of the wind. Although the beauty of a wind chime depends on the "ear of the beholder," its main purpose is always the same.

At the Communion Table we also see a unique beauty. Here, people from all walks of life and personal backgrounds come together for a single, special purpose. No matter the various "shapes, sizes, and situations" of the participants, the Lord's Supper is something beautiful.

Along with this beauty, though, is a purpose. The specific purpose of the Lord's Supper is to remind us. Remind us of what? According to Paul in 1 Corinthians 11:23-25:

> *"For I received from the Lord what I also passed on to you:*
> *The Lord Jesus, on the night he was betrayed, took bread,*
> *and when he had given thanks, he broke it and said,*
> *'This is my body, which is for you; do this in remembrance*
> *of me.' In the same way, after supper he took the cup, saying,*
> *'This cup is the new covenant in my blood; do this,*
> *whenever you drink it, in remembrance of me.'"*

The specific purpose of the Lord's Supper is to remind us of the broken body and shed blood of Christ. Why must there be blood?

> *...without the shedding of blood there is no forgiveness."*
> Hebrews 9:22

The power of the Lord's Supper is in the blood of Jesus Christ; but like a wind chime, that power must be applied to reveal the true beauty. It depends on you and your acceptance of that redeeming power.

> *"In him we have redemption through his blood...."*
> Ephesians 1:7

What makes the Lord's Supper so beautiful is that it communicates to each of us that we are saved because of His death. In this moment we are reminded of the purpose of Communion; but we also need to see its beauty: it is the blood of Jesus Christ that can energize the broken pieces of our lives with His beauty and saving power.

29
Excess Baggage

As winter approaches many of us begin to pull out our coats, gloves, snow boots, and hats so we can bundle up as we head outside in order to stay warm. But when we return to our homes, what's the first thing we do? We immediately begin to peel off all those layers of clothes and bulky accessories that were so necessary just moments before. We hang them on coatracks or in closets, or watch as the young ones just "hang" them in the middle of the floor. Why do we take off all the extra clothes? Why not leave them on so we are ready when we head back outside? The main reason is that wearing all these warm clothes makes us very uncomfortable when we're inside. Extra clothes become excess baggage that hinders us from doing what we want to do, whether it be sitting and watching television, cooking in the kitchen, or playing games with the kids. Funny how things that seemed so important (and felt so good) to us before we entered our homes are now so uncomfortable inside that we just can't keep our minds on what we are doing.

In Matthew 5:23-24 Jesus provides some guidelines on gift giving, and instructs us to be very careful what we bring to the altar with us. If we are reminded that we have offended our brother, then our gift is to be left there beside the altar. We are to first go make amends. Personal problems and conflicts must be resolved before personal sacrifices can be offered to God. All this "excess baggage" is to be shed long before we approach God. How can we have a proper relationship with God if we can't first maintain good relationships with our fellow man?

Although Jesus was probably not making a direct reference to the Communion Table in this passage, the application is still the same. When we come to the Lord's Supper with "extra baggage," such as an unforgiving spirit, a revengeful attitude, or a bitter disposition, we are not able to keep our focus on the true meaning of the Lord's Supper: love, mercy, forgiveness, and sacrifice.

> *"Therefore whoever eats the bread or drinks the cup*
> *of the Lord in an unworthy manner will be guilty of*
> *sinning against the body and blood of the Lord."*
>
> 1 Corinthians 11:27

Jesus took no excess baggage to His altar as He offered Himself as our sacrifice to God. He even asked forgiveness for His executioners! Because of His forgiving love, our burden of sin has been forever removed. At this special time Jesus now bids you remove all the extra baggage from your heart and concentrate on what we are here to do: to worship, and honor, and remember our Lord and Savior.

30
Shall We Live Again?

Socrates, the renowned Greek philosopher, devoted himself to teaching others. He encouraged self-examination of one's life and emphasized the importance of the soul. His was a life in pursuit of knowledge and wisdom, and he was successful in achieving these personal goals. However, possibly his greatest lesson was learned as he drank the poison hemlock and lay down to die. As his grief-stricken friends gathered around him here at the end, they asked "shall we live again?" The dying philosopher, full of worldly wisdom, could only reply, "I hope so, but no man can know." What a tragic response. Even after years of learning and recognition as one of the wisest teachers to ever live, there was only frustration and uncertainty here at the end. Socrates had gained the whole world, but how little he understood about the nature of his own soul.

At the Lord's Table we find little in the way of worldly wisdom. In fact, the world would probably consider the death of an innocent Sacrifice for guilty sinners as the ultimate foolishness. But, ironically, it is here that we find the answer to life's ultimate question: "shall we live again?" As we come around the Lord's Table we find the assurance that we shall indeed live again. Jesus, speaking to Martha on the occasion of Lazarus' death, had this to say:

> *"I am the resurrection and the life. He who believes* in me *will live, even though he dies...."* John 11:25

It is true that the Communion message focuses mainly on the death of Christ: His broken, battered body and His shed blood. But there is another message at this Table. As we partake, we are reminded that, yes, Christ died; but also that Jesus Christ arose from the dead!

> *"For whenever you eat this bread and drink this cup, you proclaim the Lord's death until he comes."* 1 Corinthians 11:26

Philosophers would ask how can someone who is dead return to life? But an empty tomb bears witness to the fact that Jesus Christ died and rose again. Therefore, His statement to Martha is also true. Because He is the resurrection and the life, we can live again.

Not only Easter Sunday, but every other Sunday as well, we celebrate the resurrection of Jesus. As you gather around the Lord's Table, allow this time to remind you that even though Jesus died, He is *not* dead. In Him, we find our assurance of victory over death; a victory gained through the death, burial, and resurrection of our Lord Jesus Christ.

31

A Legal Substitution

The prosecuting attorney had just completed his final summation of an airtight, irrefutable case against the accused. There was no rebuttal presented by the defense. In fact, there was no defense of any kind. No loopholes, no extenuating circumstances, no amount of legal wrangling could sway the overwhelming body of direct evidence against the defendants. This case was decidedly closed, and a final decision must now be rendered. As the accused rose to approach the bench, the Judge pronounced the only possible verdict: guilty on all counts. The sentence: death, with no hope of parole or plea bargain from this High Court. But as the bailiff escorted the condemned out of the presence of the Judge and toward final execution, a young Man suddenly stood and spoke with a compassionate, yet authoritative voice, "Wait! Take Me instead!" After a brief silence of disbelief, the Judge reminded the innocent One of the awful penalty that must be paid for transgression of the law. "I know," replied the young Man; "but I love these guilty people too much to allow them to die. If it please the court, please let Me pay their penalty." The Judge paused momentarily, then instructed the bailiff to release the prisoners and escort this bold, blameless Substitute to His death.

This courtroom drama was played out even before Adam drew his first breath. Before Jesus Christ gave life to the universe:

> *"...all things were created by him and for him."*
>
> Colossians 1:16

He determined to die so that His children might live eternally. Before He was the Creator, He was

"…the Lamb that was slain from the creation of the world."
Revelation 13:8

People cannot truly appreciate the horror of sin: its darkness and eternal separation from the light of God's presence. The absolute holiness of this Judge demands that sin's wages be paid in full, and no defense can absolve our guilt as we stand condemned before God's perfect law. Justice demands that we approach the bench of condemnation; why then do we approach a Table of celebration instead? Although we bring our sins with us, we no longer carry our deadly burden of guilt. Our trial was conducted long ago on a hill called Calvary, where the love of an innocent Sacrifice became the only defense we'll ever need. As you partake of the cup and loaf, remember that it's through the blood of Jesus Christ that our case is forever dismissed.

32
The Selfless Servant

How many of you have actually seen a wash basin? They're rather uncommon in this day and age. Today, we generally use sinks, bathtubs, and buckets to do the job of washing things; but years ago basins were where things were cleansed. In the Scriptures there is a specific mention of a basin, and also an implied use of a basin. One was used for self; one was used for others. In Matthew 27:24 we read that *"When Pilate saw that he was getting nowhere, but that instead an uproar was starting, he took water and washed his hands in front of the crowd. 'I am innocent of this man's blood,' he said."* Here the basin was used as a sign of selfishness. Pilate, who had the authority to free Jesus, instead used the basin to symbolically free himself from the responsibility of condemning an innocent Man.

But there is another basin mentioned in quite a different context. In John 13:5 we read of a quiet evening far from the noisy crowds where Jesus used a basin to cleanse others: *"After that, he* [Jesus] *poured water into a basin and began to wash his disciples' feet, drying them with the towel that was wrapped around him."* This was a basin dedicated to serving others.

As Jesus washed the feet of His apostles that night, He taught them an important lesson on servanthood. More than this single act in the Upper Room though, Jesus' life culminated in the supreme act of servanthood: giving up His life for others. When Jesus washed our sin away by dying on the cross in our place, He taught us about selfless love.

The apostle John provides us with two important lessons in 1 John 3:16-17. First, a lesson about true love:

> *"This is how we know what love is: Jesus Christ laid down his life for us. And we ought to lay down our lives for our brothers."*

Second, a lesson about true servanthood:

> *"If anyone has material possessions and sees his brother in need but has no pity on him, how can the love of God be in him?"*

And so, in a sense, we bring two basins to the Communion Table: one basin used for self, the other used just for others. How often we, in our personal lives, have chosen Pilate's basin rather than taking up the basin of Jesus. The Lord's Supper now pictures for us that His basin is one of selfless love for you and me. May we accept the commandment to love Him more by serving others. When we realize the extent of His selfless love for us, how can we not offer unselfish love to those around us?

33
The Mask

Gatlinburg is a tourist city buried deep in the heart of the Great Smoky Mountains of Tennessee. In and around Gatlinburg are many beautiful scenes that have inspired photographers and artists for years, but the most photographed sight in Gatlinburg is the not the many attractions or even the beautiful mountains. The favorite subject of cameras in Gatlinburg is in reality the sculptured head of Jesus Christ that stands in the Christus Gardens. This breathtaking marble figure of Christ is fashioned in such a way that His eyes appear to look in every direction and follow you as you walk before it. Regardless of where you stand, the eyes of Jesus Christ are upon you.

The author of Hebrews tells us:

> *"Nothing in all creation is hidden from God's sight.*
> *Everything is uncovered and laid bare before the*
> *eyes of him to whom we must give account."* Hebrews 4:13

So often we come to church trying to hide so much from each other—and sometimes even from the Lord. The word "hypocrite" actually means "mask." There are times when we all seem conveniently to wear a mask to help hide our shortcomings; to try and mask the guilt that comes from disobedience. Maybe we're even trying to fool ourselves into thinking that God will simply overlook our sin. How foolish, though, to wear a mask before the One who knows and sees all.

The suggestion as we come to the Lord's Supper is that we drop our mask before the Lord and lay our shortcomings on the Table before us. Jesus Christ placed His all on this Table. He never wears a mask. How can we do less? The Scriptures are clear that no matter what we have done or what we have become, He still loves us.

> *"But God demonstrates his own love for us in this:*
> *While we were still sinners, Christ died for us."*
> Romans 5:8

We know from John 3:16 that God loved us enough to send His son to die for us. In the story of the prodigal, or lost, son (Luke 15:20) we learn that the Father loved the son so much that he looked for him everyday to return home. No matter what the son had done the Father still loved him. The Father does not wear a mask. In 1 Corinthians 11:28 we are encouraged to examine ourselves when we come to the Communion Table:

> *"A man ought to examine himself before he*
> *eats of the bread and drinks of the cup."*

Be open with yourself and open yourself to the Lord. His eyes are always upon you as He sees and knows everything you do. Yet even when we try to mask our sin, He still loves us. Enough to die for us.

A Weekly Meal

According to an article in *The Scientist*, Dr. Albert Einstein visited Dr. Gutenberg, the senior seismologist at the California Institute of Technology in 1933. Einstein was greatly interested in the science of earthquakes, and asked many questions as they walked the campus together. Suddenly, an excited professor broke in on their conversation, and they began to notice people rushing from nearby buildings as they felt the earth moving under their feet. Dr. Gutenberg later confessed that the two scientists had become so engrossed in talking about the science earthquakes that they had failed to even notice the famous Los Angeles earthquake taking place around them.

A common concern expressed by some Christians is that Communion, if observed every Lord's Day, might lose it's meaning; it would become only a habit or ritual. Those who receive Communion monthly or even less know about the Communion, but miss the many blessings given during this special time. Those who miss Communion miss what this meal can do for them.

In the Scripture how God's people worshiped Him was a serious matter. Some were just going through the outward motions of "worship" without any inward spiritual meaning:

> *"You do not delight in sacrifice, or I would bring it;*
> *you do not take pleasure in burnt offerings. The*
> *sacrifices of God are a broken spirit; a broken and*
> *contrite heart, 0 God you will not despise."* Psalm 51:16-17

> *"Does the LORD delight in burnt offerings and sacrifices as*
> *much as in obeying the voice of the LORD? To obey is better*
> *than sacrifice, and to heed is better than the fat of rams."*
> 1 Samuel 15:22

Is it possible to take the Lord's Supper each week and have it *not* become merely "going through the motions?" According to Acts 2:42 the followers of Christ:

> *"...devoted themselves to the apostles' teaching and*
> *to fellowship, to the breaking of bread and to prayer."*

This passage teaches two things. First, early Christians exhibited a strong persistence or stubbornness in observing the Lord's Supper each time they gathered. Secondly, the apostles obviously felt Communion was of such importance that it must indeed become habitual. It was something to be shared just as often as prayer, teaching, and fellowship. Even so, the real key to observing the Lord's Supper each week is not simply how often we gather around His Table, but to center on it as the focal point of the worship experience. We expect to hear singing and sermons on any given Sunday morning, but the importance of these events pales when compared to the power of the Lord's Supper. Here is where God expects us to be. Here, we are reminded of Christ's love for you and me.

A Sharing

What does Communion mean? The word means "fellowship" or "common mind." When we come to the Communion time, with whom do we come and how are we to fellowship? The most common answer is that we fellowship with Christ as we remember His broken body, and shed blood. But how often do we consider the possibility of fellowship with each of our brothers and sisters in Christ?

Nearly four hundred years ago the English poet-clergyman John Donne wrote, "No man is an island entirely of itself; every man is a piece of the continent, a part of the main; any man's death diminishes me, because I am involved in the mainland." The poet wanted it understood that he needed people; and at the Communion time we need each other. How do we know this? Nowhere in Scripture do we find a reference to Communion being held in a setting of one individual. It is a *shared* experience.

"They devoted themselves...."

Acts 2:42

"...when you come together as a church...."

1 Corinthians 11:18

Acts 20:7 describes one of Paul's missionary journeys where they *"came together"* to break bread. Obviously, we need each other; and this is especially true during the Communion time.

Why the need to share this common bond? Just as the poet refers to us all as a "continent," Scripture refers to us as a *family*. As a family, the time around the "Table" is important for us all. It is there that we are reminded of our common bond in Christ. It is there that we are so vividly reminded of our Father and His love for us. It is there that we are reminded that we, though being individuals, have a unifying purpose: to communicate the love of our Father to others.

Maybe this is why we are told in Hebrews 10:25 that we are to continue meeting together:

"Let us not give up meeting together, as some are in the habit of doing, but let us encourage one another...."

What better place to encourage and fellowship with one another than at the "Table." As you pass the bread and the cup to your brother or sister, you might consider saying to them "Christ died for you and me."

36
Don't Blame Me!

Someone penned these words:

Ye call me Master and obey me not,
Ye call me Light and see me not,
Ye call me Way and walk me not,
Ye call me Life and desire me not,
Ye call me Wise and follow me not,
Ye call me Fair and love me not,
Ye call me Rich and ask me not,
Ye call me Eternal and seek me not,
Ye call me Gracious and trust me not,
Ye call me Noble and serve me not,
Ye call me Mighty and honor me not,
Ye call me Just and fear me not,
If I condemn you, Blame Me Not!

The first of these thoughtful lines is the most interesting, and actually summarizes the message. "Ye call me Master and obey me not." We live in a society that strives to make its own rules; where each wants to obey only himself or herself. Brides often delete the word "obey" in their marriage vows. The number of self-employed people is the highest ever, as people desire to be their own boss. What teenager hasn't at one time said "you can't tell me what to do"? A doctor will tell you that the most frustrating patient is the one who refuses to obey orders. One study actually demonstrated that nearly 90% of all patients leave half-full pill bottles, cheat on their diets, or never return for checkups despite careful prescriptions and explicit advice.

As we come to the Lord's Supper, there is a very clear command found in both Luke and 1 Corinthians. In 1 Corinthians 11:23-25 the commandment is to:

"...do this in remembrance of me."

Our command at the Communion time is that whenever we take part, we are to remember Jesus. But what if we disregard Jesus' instruction and refuse to carefully consider the true meaning of the cup and the loaf? Consider what Paul says four verses later in 1 Corinthians 11:29:

> *"For anyone who eats and drinks without recognizing the*
> *body of the Lord eats and drinks judgment on himself."*

What does the poem say again?

> *Ye call me Master and obey me not....*
> *If I condemn you, Blame Me Not!*

Does God Really Forgive?

Once upon a time, God had a problem. A big problem. His perfect holiness demanded that all sin be destroyed by His righteous wrath:

> *"...our 'God is a consuming fire.'"*
>
> Hebrews 12:29

On the other hand, His perfect love demanded that His children, although mired in sin, be forgiven to live forever with Him:

> *"He is patient with you, not wanting anyone to perish...."*
>
> 2 Peter 3:9

But how could God reconcile love and wrath—mercy with total obliteration—without violating His divine nature and perfect attributes? Just when there appeared to be no hope of finding a way to save His children, God chose to make a way. His solution? Punish the sin as required, but save the sinner by transferring the terrible penalty to a willing Substitute, Jesus Christ, the Lamb of God.

Christians speak often of being "forgiven," but that is true only in the sense that we are "released" from the penalty of our sins, much as a bow releases an arrow. God cannot overlook or neglect our sin; His very nature will not allow it. His holiness demands that all sin be accounted for and punished accordingly. The arrow of sin must eventually fall. For the Christian, however, this punishment has already been meted out on the cross. Here is the target of our arrow:

> *"God made him who had no sin to be sin for us, so that*
> *in him we might become the righteousness of God."*
> 2 Corinthians 5:21

Jesus, the Great Substitute, took the penalty of our sin upon Himself and suffered the punishment so rightly belonging to us. In exchange, we are declared righteous in God's eyes if we accept the free gift of salvation from Jesus and are immersed into Him (Romans 6:3). As we now gather around this Table of Grace, be reminded that Jesus Christ is the only link between a perfect God and an imperfect people otherwise doomed to destruction. As you partake of the bread and the cup, remember God's big problem. Be thankful for a Big Savior that solved our problem by loving us enough to experience the wrath of God.

38
The Tree of Life

A lifeless form lay before Him. Beautifully and intricately crafted, yet cold and motionless, awaiting the Master's gift of life. As He knelt down on the new green grass to bestow the eternal image of God, He paused just for a moment, knowing full well what this would one day mean. Bringing the man to life meant that He would have to die. There would be no going back, no reconsidering or rethinking the matter. Raising Adam from the dust demanded that Jesus be raised on a cross. Just then, maybe just for an instant, the Father paused there above the body and cast a loving glance toward the pre-incarnate form of Jesus. "Are You sure?" Jesus needed no words to reply. He simply smiled, and placed His hand upon Adam's shoulder with the touch of a mother holding her baby for the first time. Can you imagine the first thoughts of the man as he opened his eyes and looked into the eyes of Jesus? Could he realize he had been filled with the breath of His life and awakened to touch the hand of God?

It would have been easy for Jesus to back out. After all, why should He die for disobedient millions that would refuse to know Him, or worse, even curse His holy name? In a word, the answer is *love*.

> *"This is love: not that we loved God, but that he loved*
> *us and sent his Son as an atoning sacrifice for our sins."*
> 1 John 4:10

Because Jesus is omniscient and sees the future just as clearly as the past, He saw another tree standing in the Garden of Eden; there beside man's Tree of Life, was Jesus' tree of death. One tree, a beautiful reminder of God's gift of life to man. The other, the terrible instrument on which God gave His life for man. But are these trees really all that different? Eating fruit from the Tree of Life sustained Adam physically, but could not remove the sin that destroyed his spirit. There had to be another "tree of life" bearing another Fruit.

When we come around the Lord's Table, we partake of the symbol of Jesus' body that was nailed to a cross—the only one of Eden's trees that still bears fruit today. The cross becomes our Tree of Life when we believe in and accept the Fruit that once hung there for us. Jesus is with us now at His Table. At the foot of the cross, Jesus still reaches down to touch us and offers the Fruit of His tree of eternal life.

Separation

The Communion cup before us now is certainly here to remind us of the blood of Christ. Blood matted in His hair and running down His face from the crown of thorns and the beatings, blood on His back due to the lashing of the whip, blood on His hands and His feet due to the nails, and blood from His side where He was pierced with the spear. This awesome reminder of Jesus' blood is not just a small cup of juice laid in a golden tray for our convenience. The Communion cup brings us face to face with the death of Christ. His death on our behalf. This is the real cup we are to take up and receive, just as Jesus commanded His followers to do.

But Jesus spoke of another cup while He struggled in the Garden of Gethsemene.

> *"Going a little farther, he fell with his face to the ground and prayed, 'My Father, if it is possible, may this cup be taken from me."* Matthew 26:39

Many would say that this "cup" refers to Jesus' physical death on the cross, and that Jesus was praying that He might not have to die that terrible death. But there is another possibility. Could it be that this cup was filled with a different suffering even more terrible than the cross? Long ago Jesus had accepted that fact that His blood would be shed at Calvary. This is why He instituted the cup of the Lord's Supper. But what is this other cup of suffering?

It could very well be the suffering that Christ would have to go through when He would be separated from His Father because of our sins. That spiritual alienation from God the Father produced greater agony than any nail or spear. It was at that moment of separation that Jesus cried, *"My God, My God why have you forsaken me?"* This second cup is also a part of the Communion time because we are reminded that Christ became our sin so we could be freed from sin's penalty.

> *"God made him who had no sin to be sin for us...."*
> 2 Corinthians 5:21

Holy, perfect God leaving His throne of glory to actually become what He hates the most? God allowing Himself to be split apart and separated from The Son? What could have possibly motivated God to do this? Could it have been the certainty of spending eternity separated from the ones He loves so dearly—His children? Just as surely as the cross separated God the Father from God the Son, the cross was also the only means of uniting God the Father with His loved ones. When Jesus was forsaken, we were forgiven.

So remember the shed blood, pain, and death of Jesus Christ; but also remember a Man alone, separated, devastated by our sins. Remember *both* cups.

40
The Carpenter's Hand

In a *Slow and Certain Light,* Elizabeth Elliot tells about her father's experiences with angelic helpers:

> *My father, when he was a small boy, was climbing on an upper*

story of a house that was being built. He walked to the end of a board that was not nailed at the other end, and it slowly began to tip. He knew that he was doomed, but inexplicably the board began to tip the other way, as though a hand had pushed it down again. He always wondered if it was an angel's hand.

Many of us seek to build our lives by our own hands, using "boards" of our own making. However, God's Word has some very unsettling things to say about the material of our lives:

> *"All of us have become like one who is unclean, and all our righteous acts are like filthy rags...."*
>
> Isaiah 64:6

> *"...for all have sinned and fall short of the glory of God.... the wages of sin is death...."*
>
> Romans 3:23; 6:23

These sobering Scriptures assure us that the board we struggle to build our lives upon was slowly tipping under the weight of our sin. We were surely doomed to receive the wages we deserved. Then, just when all hope was lost, the Master Builder appeared, and the touch of His Hand tipped our board the other way. How foolish it is to try to build our own lives on our own foundation. Even the most "righteous" of people can build only what must eventually be condemned. There is only One Who can take our "filthy" boards and fashion a beautiful life—the Carpenter of Nazareth.

The Communion time reminds us that a Hand pushed the other end of our board down so that we might be saved. The remainder of verse 23 above informs us that we have been justified by the redemption that came by Jesus Christ. Very simply stated, we were lost, but now we are saved by the death of Jesus on the cross we built. Not only is this the message of the gospel that is to be proclaimed to all people; it is also the message of the Lord's Supper that is to be communicated to believers each week.

To See Him

In Philadelphia's Grace Baptist Church, Dr. Russell Conwell had these simple words inscribed upon the back of the pulpit: "We would see Jesus." Interestingly, these words were only visible to the one standing behind the pulpit, so that every time Conwell rose to preach these words reminded him of his purpose and challenged him to put his words into practice. It was his great desire to present Christ to his congregation in both word and deed.

We might not find those specific words etched in our pulpit or somewhere else in our church, but we do have an important reminder to be like Christ. Our reminder is the Communion Table, and upon many of those Tables we read these inscribed words: *This do in remembrance of me*" (*KJV*). Certainly the Communion time calls us to remember Jesus' death and suffering, but it is also a call to remember that we are to be Christlike, even to the point of dying for one another.

> *"This is how we know what love is: Jesus Christ laid down his*
> *life for us. And we ought to lay down our lives for our brothers."*
> 1 John 3:16

But you might ask, how many opportunities do I have to lay down my life for my brother or sister? Just so that we're without excuse, John answers our question in the next verse of that same chapter:

"If anyone has material possessions and sees
his brother in need but has no pity on him,
how can the love of God be in him?"

Good question!

Our Communion time reminds us that because Jesus put us first and even died for us, we also need to put others first and do all that we can to let others see Jesus in us. It is interesting to see the dynamic effect these words have on those who will listen. Evidently those inscribed words made quite a difference in the life of Dr. Conwell, for he was voted the first citizen of Philadelphia in recognition of the Christlikeness of his character in founding Temple University and Temple Hospital for the education and care of the poor.

What about you? Has Communion made a difference in your life so that people can see Jesus living through your words and deeds? The grace of the Lord's Table has the power not only to save, but also to transform lives—if you allow it to happen.

42
The Invitation You Can't Refuse

At least on two different occasions we are told in Scripture to obey and be subject to our rulers and authorities. The implication is that whoever has authority over us—our government, bosses, coaches, or parents—we are to obey their rules and directions. Our obedience is not based on how many or how few rules there are; we are to obey. Many times as children get older there are fewer household rules for them to follow; still however, the child's responsibility is always to obey.

Before you became a Christian, what rules did you obey? Who set the standard upon which you lived your life? The apostle Paul lived by quite a different set of rules before he met Jesus Christ, and he wrote of his former life in his letter to Titus:

> *"At one time we too were foolish, disobedient, deceived*
> *and enslaved by all kinds of passions and pleasures.*
> *We lived in malice and envy, being hated and hating*
> *one another. But when the kindness and love of*
> *God our Savior appeared, he saved us, not because of*
> *righteous things we had done, but because of his mercy."*
>
> Titus 3:3-5

But when we enter the church building, and especially when we gather around the Lord's Table, to what Authority do we submit? Certainly we come around the Communion Table to remember, but there's more to it than that. We come also to submit to the authority of Jesus Christ. He commands that we be here. He commands us to take the loaf and the cup. In so doing, we recognize that it is only by His authority and power that we may be saved. Because:

> *"…there is no other name under heaven*
> *given to men by which we must be saved."*
>
> Acts 4:12

How selfish of us to neglect being around Jesus' Table! If we can't come here because of love, then at least we should come here out of obedience. His love compels us, but His commands demand our presence. Let us now follow the commands of Christ. Block out everything else in our lives: block out what you're going to do after church, block out what happened yesterday, block out what that person said to you, and focus on the mercy, the love, the death, the cross of Jesus Christ.

43
Our Special Place

Some folks take getaway trips to hideaway cottages for the purpose of "hiding away" from the stress, chaos, and problems of society and their own lives. Others may not have a secret destination or out-of-town refuge, but nonetheless they do seek out and find a special place where they can disappear to and escape at least for a short time. Maybe that special place is a park near their home, a favorite restaurant, or maybe even just a swing in their own back yard. No matter the distance or degree of seclusion, these secret places serve the same purpose—to provide a getaway from life's struggles and pressures.

For Christians, however, we need not seek out a refuge miles from our everyday lives. We need only to look to God's Word for our Special Place. Over 100 times the Scriptures refer to the Lord as our refuge and fortress. Forty-four of these occurrences are mentioned by David in the Book of Psalms, with possibly Psalm 9:9 summing it up best:

"The LORD is a refuge for the oppressed,
a stronghold in times of trouble."

The Lord is our Special Place where we seek shelter and assurance from life's struggles, pains, and hurts. And what better place to find the Lord of Refuge than here at the Lord's Table. It is here that you can lay down your worries, rejections, and loneliness. There are no shoulders bigger than those of Jesus. If He carried the sins of the world upon Himself, then He can surely help lighten our burdens and sustain us in our struggles. This special Communion time reminds us that Someone loved us enough to die for us. And if He was willing to die for us, would He not sustain us in and protect us from oppression and hardships?

*"Who shall separate us from the love of Christ? Shall
trouble or hardship or persecution or famine or nakedness
or danger or sword?.... No, in all these things we are more
than conquerors through him who loved us. For I am convinced
that neither death nor life, neither angels nor demons, neither
the present nor the future, nor any powers, neither height nor
depth, nor anything else in all creation, will be able to separate
us from the love of God that is in Christ Jesus our Lord."*
                                                    Romans 8:35, 37-39

What better place to see that love of Christ than here around His
Table? What better place do we find a Refuge? What better place to
leave the cares of this world than at the Lord's Supper?

44

The Community of Believers

*"Let us not give up meeting together, as some are in
the habit of doing, but let us encourage one another—
and all the more as you see the Day approaching."*
                                                    Hebrews 10:25

Living in a subdivision has both advantages and disadvantages. There
are times when privacy is at a premium as your neighbors may often see
what you are doing. Also, the value of your own property is greatly
affected by what your neighbors have and how they take care of their
own things. On the other hand, you just may develop friendships that
last a lifetime. Even those little signs warning that a neighborhood is
protected by "community watch" say a great deal about you and your
neighbors. These signs communicate unity and concern for one anoth-

75

er, and also let people know that there is a special bond within the people of that neighborhood.

The above passage in Hebrews reminds us that we each have a special need to meet together as a collective Body of believers. Christians are to encourage each other, develop unity, share concerns, and also lean on one another for support and assistance. If simply meeting together as Christians can help develop these caring attitudes, how much more powerful and effective is meeting together as a family around the Lord's Table.

In the Book of Acts we read of this special bond that Christians have with one another; especially when we gather together at the Communion time:

> *"Every day they continued to meet together in the*
> *temple courts. They broke bread in their homes and*
> *ate together with glad and sincere hearts, praising*
> *God and enjoying the favor of all the people."*
>
> Acts 2:46-47

The word "Communion" means "fellowship," and refers to a special bond. The bond formed and sustained by the Communion feast is certainly one we have with the Lord, but it is also a special bond we share with each other. The Lord's Supper reminds us of that mutual bond. Christ did not die just for me, but for those around me as well. As we pass the bread, we remember that the body of Jesus Christ was beaten and torn for both me and my brother. As we pass the cup, we remember that the blood of Jesus was shed for my sister as well as for me. The Communion bonds me with my brothers and sisters in Christ as nothing else in the worship service does because God so loved the world that He gave His Son.

Love and Life

A few years back there was a popular song that contained this chorus, "Love will keep us alive." The song was referring to a relationship between a man and a woman, and how love would keep them going even through those difficult times. As many of us can attest to, there are times when love does indeed keep a relationship going. This idea of love's power to bond people together is not unlike our relationship with God. During those times when we go astray and fail because of our disobedience, it is His love for us that keeps Him close and gives us the opportunity to once again return to Him. Especially now at the time of Communion we are reminded of the awesome power of God's love; a love that both saves and protects. As the words suggest, it truly is His love that keeps us alive in Him.

If we change one word in the chorus of that song, it more appropriately describes what God has done for us: "Love will *make* us alive."

> *"As for you, you were dead in your transgressions and sins…. But because of his great love for us, God, who is rich in mercy made us alive with Christ even when we were dead in transgressions…."*
>
> Ephesians 2:1, 4-5

We have been made alive because of the love of God. The same idea is also expressed in Romans 6:11:

> *"In the same way count yourselves dead to sin but alive to God in Christ Jesus."*

But exactly what does it mean to have been dead, but now alive? The

Bible uses the terms "slave" and "free" as parallels for "dead" and "alive." At one time we were slaves to sin (Romans 6:6), but now have been set free from sin (Romans 6:18). Since we are free from sin, we need to live like liberated people no longer under sin's mastery. We need to live with confidence realizing that Satan has no real power over us. We need to live with joy, understanding that there is nothing that can separate us from the love of God. And we need to live victoriously for we have the promise of eternal life. Truly, it is the love of God that has made us alive. Because Jesus Christ is the only source of true life (John 11:25), only He can make us fully alive in this world and in the world to come.

At this Communion time be reminded that God loved us enough to send the Lifegiver to die. What a terrible, yet blessed paradox it is that our life could be purchased only through His death. Here at the Lord's Table we see vivid reminders that we are set free from sin in order to be a new creation and live a new life. As you partake, remember that His love has indeed made you alive.

46
Get Ready

"0, you better watch out. You better not pout. You better not cry. I'm telling you why. Santa Claus is coming to town."

This song sums up a fascinating principle exhibited throughout our lives: when we look forward to something, our attitudes and, yes, even our actions change. Everyone's calendar is marked with special days, and throughout life we look forward to a number of those special events and times. Maybe it's a play, a sporting event, or even the visit of relatives or friends we just can't wait to see. While we anxiously await that special day, we find that the closer it gets the more our actions exemplify our anticipation. A good example is the time loved ones are expect-ed. We begin preparing for their stay days ahead of time. Rooms must be cleaned. Sometimes even refrigerators must be moved so every inch of floor can be spotless for the important guests. Special foods of cele-bration must be bought and prepared. Plans are made for activities to insure that our visitors see the best of what our town has to offer. Our actions reveal our anticipation and the excitement we feel because those we love will soon be with us.

As Christians, we are anxiously to anticipate the promised visit of our Loved One. In 1 Corinthians 11:26 we are told:

> *"…whenever you eat this bread and drink this cup,*
> *you proclaim the Lord's death until he comes."*

The Communion time reminds us of that day we so eagerly await— the day of the Lord's return. And if we truly do await the Lord's return, then it will affect our actions every day of our lives. We will make plans to "get our house in order," and seek to remove the dirt of sin that tar-nishes our lives. Although we can't mark the day of His return on our calendars, this Visitor does not come completely unannounced. When He arrives, however, it is He who will do the cleaning.

> *"But the day of the Lord will come like a thief. The heavens will*
> *disappear with a roar, the elements will be destroyed by fire,*
> *and the earth and everything in it will be laid bare. Since*
> *everything will be destroyed in this way, what kind of people*
> *ought you to be? You ought to live holy and godly lives as*
> *you look forward to the day of God and speed its coming."*
> 2 Peter 3:10-12

Use this time around His Table to remember that the Lord is coming back. We come not just to remember a death, but to prepare for an arrival. Although Communion is a time of memorial, it is also a time of

"Maranatha" (*marana tha*, literally, "Our Lord, come!"). Here, we certainly remember the past, but we also look to the future. But what about the *present*? If we really await Jesus' return, we need to be ready to present Him with holy and pure lives. Are you preparing to meet Jesus? What will He find in your spiritual house?

47
The Ultimate Victory

One of the strangest unsolved mysteries on record describes a set of peculiar hoof prints found in the snow of Devonshire, England, on the morning of February 9, 1855. These prints were oval, about the size of a donkey's hoof, and preceded each other eight inches apart in a direct line imitating a tightrope walker. The tracks covered a distance of 98 miles, passed through 15 towns, and crossed a river. In some cases the prints even ran up the side of a house or barn, over the roof, and continued on the other side. When befuddled scientists concluded that no living creature could possibly have left such prints, the rumor spread among the townspeople in the area that these tracks could only have been made by the devil himself. Consequently many superstitious people were afraid to go outdoors after dark for months in the wake of this mysterious visitor.

No matter what you believe or think about the devil, what he looks like, what his powers are, this one fact is sure: Satan has been defeated by the resurrection of Jesus Christ. The Communion time reminds us of that ultimate victory. In the Garden of Eden when God was handing out the consequences to those who participated in the first sin, He told the serpent:

> *"And I will put enmity between you and the woman,*
> *and between your offspring and hers; he will crush*
> *your head, and you will strike his heel."* Genesis 3:15

This was a prophecy fulfilled at the death and resurrection of Christ. When Jesus died, Satan was dealt the final death blow. To be sure, Satan had struck the heel of the woman's Offspring. But when Jesus arose three days later He had not only defeated Satan, but also destroyed death itself. In Scripture, death is referred to as the "last enemy." The empty tomb stands as a witness not only to the fact that Jesus arose, but also to the certainty that the death has been forever emptied of its power. That is why in 1 Corinthians 15:55 Paul cries out:

"Where, 0 death, is your victory? Where, 0 death, is your sting?"

Jesus Christ died, but rose again. The real casualty of Calvary was death and Satan's temporary power over us. What does all this have to do with the Lord's Supper? Earlier Paul says this in reference to the partaking of Communion:

"For whenever you eat this bread and drink this cup,
you proclaim the Lord's death until he comes."
1 Corinthians 11:26

The Lord's Supper reminds us that Jesus died, but it also demonstrates that He is alive, He arose, He is victorious, He crushed the head of Satan, and He is coming back for you and me, His children. Communion is a time of assurance that Jesus' victory over death has been miraculously transformed into a victory celebration for God's people today!

48
Words from the Table

Let's now focus on some important words the Lord's Supper communicates to you and me.

LOVE

> *"Greater love has no one than this,*
> *that he lay down his life for his friends."*
>
> John 15:13

> *"For God so loved the world that he gave his one and only Son...."*
>
> John 3:16

MERCY

> *"Praise be to the God and Father of our Lord Jesus Christ!*
> *In his great mercy he has given us new birth into a living*
> *hope through the resurrection of Jesus Christ from the dead...."*
>
> 1 Peter 1:3

> *"...he saved us, not because of righteous things*
> *we had done, but because of his mercy."*
>
> Titus 3:5

COMPASSION

> *"When he saw the crowds, he had compassion*
> *on them, because they were harassed and*
> *helpless, like sheep without a shepherd."*
>
> Matthew 9:36

> *"We all, like sheep, have gone astray, each*
> *of u has turned to his own way; and the LORD*
> *has laid on him the iniquity of us all."*
>
> Isaiah 53:6

> *"The Lord is full of compassion and mercy."*
>
> James 5:11

FORGIVENESS

> *"In fact, the law requires that nearly everything*
> *be cleansed with blood, and without the*
> *shedding of blood there is no forgiveness."* Hebrews 9:22

> *"This is my blood of the covenant, which is*
> *poured out for many for the forgiveness of sins."*
> Matthew 26:28

SACRIFICE

> *"...live a life of love, just as Christ loved us and gave*
> *himself up for us as a fragrant offering and sacrifice God."*
> Ephesians 5:2

> *"He is the atoning sacrifice for our sins, and not*
> *only for ours but for the sins of the whole world."*
> 1 John 2:2

> *"This is love: not that we loved God, but that he loved*
> *us and sent his Son as an atoning sacrifice for our sins."*
> 1 John 4:10

In an amazing, almost miraculous way the Communion reminds us of all these things: the Lord's Love, Mercy, Compassion, Forgiveness, and Sacrifice for you and me.

49
Loss of a Loved One

Many people consider a dog to be man's best friend. Yours might be a cat, bird, or pot-bellied pig. It is certainly true that human beings tend to develop a loving relationship with their pets. We care for them, feed them, groom them, provide for their every need, and in some strange way they become a part of our family. So much so, that for some the sorrow that comes with the loss of a pet is as great as they would feel at the loss of a close friend, or possibly even a family member. Often times older folks experience great depression at the death of their pets. Some people even go to the extreme of purchasing cemetery plots for their deceased animals. The bonding of an animal to a person is hard to explain, but nonetheless very real.

In Exodus 12 God gave the instructions for the first Passover to the Israelites. Most Christians know that the instructions for this night involved killing of the Passover lamb; yet many of us continue to over-look the unusual instruction of God in verse 6 of that chapter. Each family was to select an unblemished male animal on the tenth day of month. The act of sacrifice, however, would not occur until twilight of the four-teenth day. What we tend to forget is the simple math involved in God's Passover equation: the family was to live with the young animal four days.

"Take care of them [the lambs] *until the fourteenth day of the month, when all the people of the community of Israel must slaughter them at twilight."*

Why would God specify this four-day delay before the killing would occur? Although we're not told specifically why, it is likely that during those four days the family, especially the children, would become very attached to the "new family member." Quite probably, the little animal would have even been given a name. Nevertheless, in order for the rest of the family to be saved from the certainty of death on that Passover night, they killed that little lamb and placed its blood on their door-frames. How hard, do you think, it must have been to slaughter that innocent lamb?

Are we possibly being reminded of how God must have felt about allowing His innocent Son to be murdered in place of sinners who really deserved the punishment? Often times we focus on the great sacrifice Jesus made when He gave His life on the cross, as well we should; but maybe we need to remember that it was God Who developed His plan of salvation and set it into motion. His plan included His only Son dying so we might be saved.

"Look, the Lamb of God, who takes away the sin of the world!"
John 1:29

As we gather around the Table that reminds us our penalty has "passed over" us, remember the love and sacrifice of Jesus; but be sure and not forget the love and sacrifice of God the Father for you and me.

50
Our Peace Treaty

We hear a lot about "peace" and "peace treaties in our world today. Here are some disturbing facts about the effectiveness of mankind's attempts at forging a lasting peace. From the year 1500 BC to AD 1860 more than 8,000 treaties of peace, meant to remain in force forever, were either violated or broken entirely. Sadly, the average life span of a peace treaty was only two short years. Since as recently as 1919, the nations of Europe have signed more than 200 treaties of peace. Despite these good intentions, each treaty was broken far more easily than it was consummated.

Why is there no peace on earth? Our problem results from the fact that the world's "solution" for peace is indeed different from the concept of "peace" clearly outlined in God's Word. The world understands peace to mean an absence of conflict. In contrast, Scripture teaches that peace can be found only in the presence of God. Our peace, in reality, is in our relationship with God. Jesus said,

> *"Peace I leave with you; my peace I give you.*
> *I do not give to you as the world gives."*
>
> John 14:27

Jesus' peace was different from that of the world. He desired to give us the secret for the soul's true inner peace that we needed more than anything else: a restored relationship with God the Father. The Scriptures refer to this as reconciliation:

> *"For God was pleased to have all his fullness dwell*
> *in him, and through him to reconcile to himself all*
> *things, whether things on earth or things in heaven,*
> *by making peace through his blood, shed on the cross."*
>
> Colossians 1:19-20

We are told in Scripture that all of us were separated from God by our sin. Isaiah reminds us of this truth:

> *"Surely the arm of the LORD is not too short to save,*
> *nor his ear too dull to hear. But your iniquities have*
> *separated you from your God; your sins have hidden*
> *his face from you, so that he will not hear."*
>
> Isaiah 59:1-2

The peace we received from Jesus was in the forgiveness of our sins, removed by His death on the cross, so we might experience a proper relationship with God the Father. As we focus on the death of Christ at this Communion time, let's remember that we have been reconciled, restored, and renewed in our relationship with our God.

51

Enjoying Judgment Day

Judgment Day is one of the most misunderstood topics of the Bible. Ironically, Christians, who have had their sins forgiven, are often more worried about the implications of Judgment Day than are the agnostics. We who believe God's Word understand that

> *"...we will all stand before God's judgment seat."*
> Romans 14:10

What scares many is that we are well aware of "what is due" us. As sinners, it is true that we have "earned" death (Romans 6:23), but as those who have trusted their salvation to the blood of Jesus Christ, we also understand that our sins have been forgiven. Still, the thought of one day standing before Christ's judgment seat is uncomfortable, to say the least. Is there still some doubt about our eternal destiny? Because Jesus is a righteous, fair Judge, how then can we possibly escape receiving what we've so richly earned?

What many of us fail to realize is that our salvation is not in question at the judgment seat. Instead, the works we've performed during our lifetime will be judged for their eternal significance.

> *"... fire will test the quality of each man's work. If what*
> *he has built survives, he will receive his reward. If it is*
> *burned up, he will suffer loss; he himself will be saved."*
> 1 Corinthians 3:13-15

The Christian may, therefore, approach the Judgment Seat of Christ with confidence and without fear. But from what do we derive our confidence, and what has removed our fear? We need only to look to the Lord's Table to find the eternal answers to these questions. It is here that we find tangible proofs of the love of God—His perfect love that removes any fear from our hearts.

> *"...we will have confidence on the day of judgment....*
> *There is no fear in love. But perfect love drives out*
> *fear, because fear has to do with punishment. The*
> *one who fears is not made perfect in love."*
> 1 John 4:17-18

Our fear has been driven away by the perfect love of God. A love so strong that it held Jesus Christ on a cross. A love so powerful that it raised Jesus Christ from the dead. A love so penetrating that it reached into our hearts and removed not only our sin, but also the threat of pending judgment. As you now receive His cup and the loaf, remember that it was Jesus Who received your judgment.

52
Justice Has Been Served

It seems that any new philosophy or "religion" is readily accepted in today's modern society; any, that is, except one that stands upon the foundational truths of God's Word. If a person believes in Biblical inerrancy and calls a sin "a sin," that person is immediately branded as "intolerant" or espousing a philosophy of "hate." The real irony about this matter, however, is that those who consider Christians to be "intolerant" fail to realize just how tolerant God really is. The apostle Paul tells us in Romans 3:25 that God has actually been so patient with us as to leave some sins temporarily unpunished.

> *"God presented him* [Jesus Christ] *as a sacrifice of atonement, through faith in his blood. He did this to demonstrate his justice, because in his forbearance he had left the sins committed beforehand unpunished—"*

The problem is that people often have a tendency to confuse God's amazing patience for divine blindness. God continues to withhold final punishment because He is waiting for all, even those who tolerate sin, to come to repentance.

> *"The Lord is not slow in keeping his promise, as some understand slowness. He is patient with you, not wanting anyone to perish, but everyone to come to repentance. But the day of the Lord will come like a thief.... Since everything will be destroyed in this way, what kind of people ought you to be? You ought to live holy and godly lives as you look forward to the day of God."*
>
> 2 Peter 3:9, 11

How can a just God delay punishment? He doesn't really. God has already demonstrated His full justice before all of humanity—on the cross. Here is the dual purpose of Calvary: to witness for all time that a *just* God cannot and will not leave any sin unpunished, and to provide the means of *justifying* you and me—if we accept the justifying grace of God freely given through the substitutionary death of Jesus Christ.

When we come around the Lord's Table, we come to a powerful reminder that God is both Just and the One Who Justifies. The two inseparable emblems on this Table also serve to remind us of two inseparable attributes of God: His great love and His great wrath against sin. Just now, consider the great price that God paid to transform enemies deserving His wrath into His children who can now receive His love and mercy.

Scripture Index

Scripture Index

Subject/Name Index

Abel, 46,50

Abraham Lincoln, 47

Adam (Eve), 25,56,67

apostle(s),
33,39,48,58,61,62,72,88

assure, assurance,
15,55,70,74,81

atonement, 22,89

betray, betrayed, 13,52

blood, bloodstream,
15,16,19,20,21,24,26,27,28,
29,32,35,37,38,52,55,62,68,
69,76,84,86,87,89

body [Jesus'],
15,22,24,25,40,41,49,52,54,
62,65,67,76
[the church], 40,65,76

bread (the)
13,15,20,24,25,40,45,46,47,
49,52,54,55,60,61,63,66,76,
79,81

breaking of bread, 25,61

Cain, 46,50

Calvary('s),
15,20,26,43,57,68,81,89

child('s), children('s),
grandchildren,
14,17,18,22,23,25,26,29,30,
39,42,43,47,56,65,69,72,81,
84,89

Christ,
15,16,19,20,21,22,23,25,26,
29,30,31,32,33,34,36,37,38,
39,41,42,44,45,46,49,52,55,

56,57,58,59,60,61,62,63,66,
68,69,70,71,73,75,76,77,78,
80,81,82,83,86,87,88,89

Christus Gardens, 59

cleanse, cleansed,
14,19,46,57,58,83

command(s), commandment(s),
32,41,58,64,68,73

communion,
15,18,21,23,26,29,30,31,32,
33,34,36,37,38,41,46,49,51,
52,53,55,58,60,61,62,63,64,
68,70,71,72,74,76,77,78,79,
80,81,83,86

contract, 20

covenant, 20,21,27,32,42,52,83

cross (the)
15,19,20,22,23,26,27,28,35,
43,44,45,48,49,51,52,55,56,
62,67,68,69,70,71,73,75,78,
79,81,84,86,87,89

crucifixion, 15

cup (the)
15,16,20,22,23,26,27,28,35,
43,44,45,46,47,48,51,52,54,
55,57,60,63,65,66,68,69,67,
73,76,79,81,88

death,
13,15,16,24,25,26,27,34,37,
43,44,45,48,49,51,52,55,56,
62,67,68,69,70,71,73,75,78,
79,81,84,86,87,89

debt, debtor, debt-free, 21,22,30

disciple('s), discipline,
17,24,25,27,58

93

Subject/Name Index

Subject/Name Index

meal, 19,23,24,27,38,51,60,61

mercy,
19,30,31,54,65,73,77,82,
83,89

Messiah, 24

miracle(s), miraculous,
13,22,28,35,42,44,45,81,83

new covenant, 20,27,32,52

Passover, 24,27,84

Paul,
18,29,33,45,48,49,52,63,65,
72,81,88
pay, payment, paid, paying,
18,20,21,22,26,30,32,38,42,
56,57,89

Peter, 24,38,45

power(s), powerful,
16,24,27,28,29,32,40,41,45,
48,51,52,62,72,73,75,77,78,
80,81,88,89

presence, 18,19,56,57,73,86

promise(s), promised,
15,22,27,29,78,79,89

reconcile(d), reconciling,
reconciliation,
13,15,41,65,86

remember, remembered,
remembering,
14,15,17,18,19,22,23,25,28,
30,31,32,33,41,45,47,49,50,
51,54,57,62,64,66,69,71,73,
76,78,80,85,86,88

remembrance,
15,30,31,52,64,71

resurrection, 45,55,80,81,82

righteous, righteousness,
16,19,32,34,36,37,42,65,66,
70,73,82,87

Robert E. Lee, 33

Ronald Reagan, 47

sacrifice(s), sacrificial,
19,22,25,30,50,51,53,54,55,
57,61,67,83,84,85,89

salvation,
14,23,27,32,36,48,66,85,87

Savior, 16,21,38,44,49,54,66,73

selfish(ness), 15,57,58,73

substitute, substitution(ary),
15,56,66,89

traitor, 13,14

transform, transformation,
16,29,35,37,72,81,89

victory, victories, (triumph),
14,15,19,55,78,80,81

wine, 27

About the Authors

James A. Joiner has been married to Lisa for 18 years. Together they have two teenage daughters, Hope and Joy. He serves as pulpit minister for Twin Tiers Christian Church in Painted Post, New York and has held ministries in Florida, Georgia, North Carolina, and Alabama. He graduated from Florida Christian College with a Bachelor's Degree and from Kentucky Christian College with a Masters of Ministry. He also is Adjunct Professor at Corning Community College in the area of Public Communication.

Richard E. White was born in Johnson City, Tennessee in 1959, and received his B.S. degree in Biology from Emory University in Atlanta, in 1981. He went on to earn his Ph.D. degree in Pharmacology from the Medical College of Georgia in 1987, and is currently an Associate Professor of Pharmacology and Toxicology at MCG in Augusta. He has been a member of the Christian Church since 1968 and is currently an elder and Sunday school teacher at Westside Christian Church, Martinez, Georgia. He and his wife, Margene, have 2 children: Gina and Daniel.